Poptropica English

STUDENT BOOK  5

Ice Island

Laura Miller • John Wiltshier
Series advisor: David Nunan

Pearson Education Limited
Edinburgh Gate
Harlow
Essex CM20 2JE
England
and Associated Companies throughout the world.

Poptropica English

© Pearson Education Limited 2015

Based on the work of Laura Miller

The rights of Laura Miller, and John Wiltshier to be identified as authors of this work have been asserted by them in accordance with the Copyright, Designs and Patents Act 1988.

Stories on pages 6–7, 16, 28, 40, 52, 64, 76, 88, and 100 by Catherine Prentice. The rights of Catherine Prentice to be identified as authors of this work have been asserted by them in accordance with the Copyright, Designs and Patents Act 1988.

Phonics syllabus and activities by Rachel Wilson

Editorial, design, and project management by hyphen

First published 2015

ISBN: 978-1-292-09125-9

Set in Fiendstar 13/16pt

Printed in China

Illustrators: Charlotte Alder (The Bright Agency), Illias Arahovitis (Beehive Illustration), Fred Blunt, Lawrence Christmas, Leo Cultura, Mark Draisey, John Martz, Rob, McClurkan (Beehive), Ken Mok, Zaharias Papadopoulos (hyphen), Dickie Seto, Christos Skaltsas (hyphen) and Olimpia Wong.

Picture Credits: The publisher would like to thank the following for their kind permission to reproduce their photographs: (Key: b-bottom; c-center; l-left; r-right; t-top)
123RF.com: 43 (trumpet), Arvind Balaraman 47 (boy), Leslie Banks 97/3, berlinimpressions 93/4, Zamfir Cristian 66tc, djem 42l (Theater), gstockstudio 90b, Bogdan Ionescu 67/3, Jose Manuel Gelpi Diaz 34 (a), 58/3, 66br, 94/1, 106/5, Mr.Yongyut Kasawong 62 (h), Teresa Kasprzycka 70 (Lily), Manav Lohia 51 (boy), manfredxy 70/3, Tyler Olson 53/2, racorn 34 (d), 58b, Jason Stitt 12/3, Igor Vorobyov 27c; Alamy Images: Art Reserve 19 (B), Aurora Photos 70/2, Bildagentur-online 103 (b), ClassicStock 102 (b), Chris Cooper-Smith 93/6, Deco 93/1, Dinodia Photos 47b, Michael Dwyer 43 (violins), Chuck Franklin 42l (Sports), Johnny Greig 43t, Heritage Image Partnership Ltd 103 (c), Horizons WWP 55l, 55r, Image Source Salsa 23tl, Images of Africa Photobank 94 (b), 94/3, David Kilpatrick 31tc, Vehbi Koca 104 (b), David L. Moore - Lifestyle 103 (a), Loop Images Ltd 66tr, Masterpics 19 (A), oh man 62 (a), Myrleen Pearson 97/2, Peter Titmuss 102 (a), WENN Ltd 46b, Jim West 42r (Theater), Janine Wiedel Photolibrary 91t, Emma Wood 47tl, ZUMA Press, Inc 79; Corbis: Picturenet / Blend Images 18t; Datacraft Co Ltd: 21; Fotolia.com: aleksandrn 62 (d), aruba2000 82 (a), bergamont 82 (d left), bluebat 61 (5/7), charger_v8 61 (6/8), Dmitry Chulov 47tr, Gordon Clark 90 (a), demidoff 61 (5/9), Kevin Eaves 51 (b), ekaterina_belova 56 (6b), fresh_water 67 (a), gosphotodesign 33 (Alex), heijotheone 41r, HSN 67/1, Svetlana Ignatenko 82 (c right), iofoto 22tr, jaggat 38l, jkphoto69 82 (b), JoLin 63/3, Alexandra Karamyshev 61 (5/3), 82 (e), Kayros Studio 61 (5/6), Khvost 61 (6/6), 82 (c left), kistya 94 (a), Dmytro Korolov 51 (e), leungchopan 33 (Alice), Pavel Losevsky 94/2, ludmilafoto 61 (6/7), Anna Lurye 63/1, michaeljung 12/2, Dudarev Mikhail 51 (d), noel moore 56 (1a), Paul Murphy 56 (6a), naluwan 106/4, Oculo 56 (1b), Pakhnyushchyy 51 (c), paleka 61 (5/1), paylessimages 56 (2a), Premat 56 (3a), promesaartstudio 56 (1b flag), Eduardo Rivero 49tl, SeanPavonePhoto 56 (2b), SergiyN 41l, Valery Shanin 90 (c), siraphol 82 (d right), sirikorn_t 70 (Bao), suprunvitaly 61 (5/8), titelio 62 (c), Alexander Trinitatov 47 (girl), Tomasz Trojanowski 37, TTstudio 56 (4b), vgstudio 12/5 & 7, Vitalinka 22bl, Lisa F. Young 93t; Getty Images: blue jean images 23tr, 23br, Carmen Martínez Banús 93/3, Jaume Gual 31tl, Image Bank / Brooke Slezak 97/7, Don Mason 94 (c), Caiaimage / Tom Merton 91b, Nivek Neslo 78, Bill Pugliano 46t, Carl Schneider 34 (b), 58/1; Imagemore Co., Ltd: 56 (2a flag), 61 (6/4); Pearson Education Ltd: Studio 8 18b, 51 (girl), 54, 59, Jon Barlow 27b, 105, 107l, Sophie Bluy 11, Gareth Boden 27t, 91c, Jörg Carstensen 106/3, Trevor Clifford 26, 34 (Amy), 58t, 66bl, 106/1, Rob Judges 15, Miguel Domínguez Muñoz 70 (Silvia), Sozaijiten 31tr, 61 (6/3); PhotoDisc: Photolink 49tr; Photolibrary. com: B2M Productions. Photodisc. 14; Shutterstock.com: 300dpi 61 (6/5), aldegonde 43 (drums), Aaron Amat 61 (6/2), Galyna Andrushko 67 (b), Leah-Anne Thompson 104 (c), Nikola Bilic 62 (g), Ingvar Bjork 61 (6/1), cabania 46 (girl), charnsitr 56 (1a flag), Coprid 63/2, Excellent backgrounds 61 (5/5), Fotokostic 53/1, Gelpi JM 39, 107r, Globe Turner 56 (2b flag), John Gomez 104 (d), Goodluz 12/6 & 7, Michelle Donahue Hillison 102 (d), Hogan Imaging 25t, holbox 106/2, HomeArt 62 (b), Stuart Jenner 104 (a), Junial Enterprises 38r, K. Miri Photography 63/4, Simon Krzic 53/3, Ivan Kuzmin 90 (b), Tom Lester 93/2, Monkey Business Images 33 (Sue), 43 (piano), Luciano Mortula 51 (a), naluwan 97/4, Tony Northrup 56 (5a), Alexandre Nunes 33 (Max), oksix 61 (5/2), oliveromg 53/4, Anna Omelchenko 12/8, ostill 34 (c), 58/2, 66bc, Ioannis Pantzi 12/1, Cyril Papot 70/1, paulaphoto 97/5, Pavel L Photo and Video 66tl, Catalin Petolea 42r (Sports), 87, PhotoNAN 61 (5/4), sculpies 56 (5b), SergiyN 29, 106/6, Artazum and Iriana Shiyan 22br, Ljupco Smokovski 97/1, Brigida Soriano 56 (4a), SSokolov 56 (3b), Stock Avalanche 25b, Syda Productions 67 (c), Patrizia Tilly 93/5, tratong 49tc, wavebreakmedia 77, Tracy Whiteside 46 (boy), Lisa F Young 12/4; www. imagesource.com: 17

All other images © Pearson Education

Contents

Scope and sequence

Welcome

Vocabulary:	**Time:** two days ago, yesterday, today, now, tomorrow
Structures:	I played tennis on Monday morning. We cleaned our rooms on Saturday morning. He/She danced at the party on Friday evening. They went to the movies on Saturday afternoon.

1 Friends

Vocabulary:	**Physical appearance:** dark hair, light hair, spiky hair, bald, handsome, beautiful, good-looking, cute **Adjectives to describe personality:** bossy, creative, sporty, lazy, smart, patient, talkative, helpful, friendly, hard-working	**Cross-curricular:** **Art:** Warm and cool colors **Values:** Help your friends in class.
Structures:	What does he/she look like? He's/She's good-looking. He/She has straight, dark hair and brown eyes. What do they look like? They're tall and good-looking. They have short, light hair and blue eyes. He/She doesn't have light hair. They don't have light hair. What's he/she like? He's sporty and he's smart. She's bossy but hard-working. I like him because he's patient. I like her because she's friendly.	

2 My life

Vocabulary:	**Daily activities:** brush my teeth, make my bed, wash my face, clean my room, do my homework, meet my friends, study before a test, take notes in class, take out the trash, be on time **Adverbs of frequency:** always, usually, often, sometimes, never	**Cross-curricular:** **Social science:** Being healthy **Values:** Giving is great.
Structures:	You must brush your teeth. *(Order)* You should brush your teeth. *(Advice)* I always brush my teeth. / He usually brushes his teeth. / She often brushes her teeth. / They sometimes brush their teeth. / We never brush our teeth.	

3 Free time

Vocabulary:	**Activities and hobbies:** hitting, kicking, throwing, catching, diving, going shopping, telling jokes, reading poetry, jumping on the trampoline **More activities and hobbies:** playing video games, in-line skating, playing chess, playing the drums, acting, singing karaoke, running races, singing in a choir	**Cross-curricular:** **Music:** Musical instruments **Values:** It's good to try new things. You should have a hobby.
Structures:	What am I good at? I'm good at hitting. What's he/she good at? He's/She's good at hitting. What are they good at? They're good at hitting. He/She isn't good at catching. / They aren't good at catching. What does he/she like/love doing? He/She likes/loves going shopping. What were you doing yesterday at 7:00? I was drawing pictures. What was he/she doing yesterday at 7:00? He/She was drawing pictures. What were they doing yesterday at 7:00? They were drawing pictures. Were you drawing pictures? Yes, I was. / No, I wasn't. Was he/she drawing pictures? Yes, he/she was. / No, he/she wasn't. Were they drawing pictures? Yes, they were. / No, they weren't.	

④ Around the world

Vocabulary:	**Countries:** China, Korea, Japan, Australia, the United States, Mexico, Colombia, Brazil, Argentina, the United Kingdom, Spain, Italy, Egypt, India **Places:** pyramid, statue, cave, volcano, city, town, farm, factory, castle	Cross-curricular: Geography: Seasons Values: Teamwork is important.
Structures:	There's a rain forest in Brazil. / There isn't a rain forest in Korea. There are some penguins in Argentina. / There aren't any penguins in Italy. Is there a pyramid in the city? Yes, there is. / No, there isn't. Are there any beaches in Australia? Yes, there are some beautiful beaches in Australia. Are there any volcanoes in the United Kingdom? No, there aren't.	

⑤ Shopping

Vocabulary:	**Clothing and accessories:** jacket, swimsuit, watch, bracelet, wallet, handbag, umbrella, gloves, sunglasses, hoodie, belt **Adjectives to describe clothing and accessories:** cheap, expensive, tight, baggy, old-fashioned, modern	Cross-curricular: Science: Properties of materials Values: Dress correctly for each occasion.
Structures:	How much is this/that jacket? It's ninety dollars and fifty cents. How much are these/those sunglasses? They're thirty dollars. Whose watch is this? It's Maddy's/mine/yours/his/hers. Whose pens are these? They're Dan's/mine/yours/his/hers.	

⑥ Party time

Vocabulary:	**Irregular past tense verbs:** make/made, have/had, come/came, give/gave, get/got, sing/sang, bring/brought, meet/met, eat/ate, see/saw **Ordinal numbers:** first, second, third, fourth, fifth, sixth, seventh, eighth, ninth, tenth, eleventh, twelfth, thirteenth, fourteenth, fifteenth, sixteenth, seventeenth, eighteenth, nineteenth, twentieth, thirtieth	Cross-curricular: History: The first Thanksgiving Values: Be a creative problem solver.
Structures:	I made a cake. / I didn't make a cake. Where did you go? I went to Ghana. When did you go to Ghana? I went on August 1st. What did you see? I saw giant butterflies. Who did you meet? I met my relatives.	

⑦ School

Vocabulary:	**Adjectives:** interesting, boring, exciting, scary, funny, difficult, easy, romantic, relaxing **School subjects:** computer science, math, geography, science, history, art, music, P.E.	Cross-curricular: Social science: Life experiences Values: Learn about your older family members' youths.
Structures:	Was it interesting? Yes, it was. / No, it wasn't. Was there an alien in it? Yes, there was. / No, there wasn't. Were there any exciting stories? Yes, there were. / No, there weren't. Did you have computer science on Tuesday? Yes, I did. / No, I didn't. Was P.E. relaxing? Yes, it was. / No, it wasn't. It was difficult.	

⑧ Entertainment

Vocabulary:	**Nationalities:** Chinese, Korean, Japanese, Australian, American, Mexican, Colombian, Brazilian, Argentinian, British, Spanish, Italian, Egyptian, Indian **Occupations:** cowboy, king, queen, scientist, spy, soldier, sailor, waiter, actor, musician	Cross-curricular: Technology: Video games Values: Be a good role model for others.
Structures:	Is he/she from the United States? Yes, he/she is. / No, he/she isn't. Where's he/she from? He's/She's from Argentina. He's/She's Argentinian. Where are they from? They're from Australia. They're Australian. He's a cowboy. He likes playing the guitar. He's a cowboy who likes playing the guitar. It's an American movie. It's very famous. It's an American movie that's very famous.	

Welcome

1 🎧 A:02 Talk about the pictures.
Then listen and read.

IT IS NIGHT ON ICE ISLAND. HECTOR FROST IS AT HOME.

Smith!

My diamonds and I...

Ah, those beautiful diamonds! I want those diamonds, Smith.

Yes, boss.

Yap!

The Queen has incredible diamonds. Where are the diamonds, Smith?

They're in the town, boss.

Not for long. Ha, ha, ha!

SMITH IS TAKING THE DIAMONDS.

Classy!

Ha, ha! Good job, Smith! They're MY diamonds now!

Yes, boss.

BANG

What was THAT?!

BANG

Lesson 1

Can understand a story

7

Hey, Mike. Hi, Gizmo.

Yo, Polly.

Rrrohh!

8

POLLY AND MIKE ARE HELPING AT THE STORE.

Please put these newspapers on the shelf.

OK, Mom.

Sure, Mrs. Jones.

9

Hey, look at this.

Wow! Mike, this is a job for the Ice Detectives.

Who?

Us, of course! You, me, and Gizmo!

ICE ISLAND NEWS

WHO HAS THE DIAMONDS?

10

Can you see anything?

No.

11

What's that, Gizmo?

It's a ribbon! It's like the ribbon in the newspaper!

Woof!

12

That's the skidoo!

Quick! Follow it!

2 **Listen and number.**

a

Hector Frost ☐

b

Smith ☐

c

Polly ☐

d

Mike ☐

e

Gizmo ☐

f

Polly's mom ☐

g

The Queen of Ice Island ☐

3 **Listen again and write.**

> clothes   diamonds   helpful   skidoo   soccer   think   TV

1   This is ___Polly___. She likes to _____ and solve problems.

2   This is _____. He likes dogs, money, and _____.

3   This is _____. He loves Mike and is very _____.

4   This is the _____. She wears diamonds and is often on _____.

5   This is _____. He likes adventure and is good at _____.

6   This is _____. He likes working out and driving a _____.

7   This is _____. She sells _____ and is good at cooking.

Can identify characters in a story

4 **Listen and match.**

A:05

1 gets up   **3** cleans his room   **5** goes swimming

2 eats lunch   **4** meets friends

5 Write.

1 She is _____ .
2 He is _____ .
3 _____
4 _____
5 _____
6 _____
7 _____ a rocket.
8 _____

6 **Look at Jenny's schedule for last week and write.**

A:06

LOOK!

I played tennis on Monday morning.

We cleaned our rooms on Sunday morning.

He/She danced at the party on Friday evening.

They went to the movies on Saturday afternoon.

My schedule

	Monday	Tuesday	Wednesday	Thursday	Friday
morning	study	study	study	study with Dylan	study
afternoon	study	play video games	play tennis with Finn	practice the piano	study
evening	practice the piano	watch TV	listen to music	go to the movies	watch TV

1 She ___practiced___ the piano on Monday evening and Thursday afternoon.

2 She _____ video games on Tuesday afternoon.

3 She _____ to music on Wednesday evening.

4 She _____ with Dylan on Thursday morning.

5 She _____ to the movies on Thursday evening.

6 She _____ TV on Friday evening.

TIP!

listen	listened
play	played
practice	practiced
study	studied
watch	watched
go	went

See more on page 116.

7  A:07 **Listen and number. Then write.**

a

b

c

d

e

f

a She _____ her room.

b They _____ badminton.

c They _____ TV.

d I _____ the piano.

e He _____ to school.

f We _____ at school.

Can identify when people did activities in the past

8 **Listen and say.**

Now

two days ago	yesterday	today	tomorrow
Saturday	Sunday	Monday	Tuesday

9 **Listen and read.**

Now it's 10 o'clock.   Yesterday was Sunday.
Today is Monday.   Two days ago was Saturday.
Tomorrow is Tuesday.

10 **Write.**

Now it's three o'clock.

1 Now it's _____.
2 Today is _____.
3 Tomorrow is _____.
4 Yesterday was _____.
5 Two days ago was _____.

11 **Listen and match. Then write.**

1    **2**    **3**    **4**

(two weeks ago)   (three years ago)   (yesterday)   (two days ago)

1 I _____ that _____.
2 I _____.
3 We _____.
4 I _____.

12 **Talk about yourself.**

I walked to school yesterday.

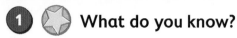

Friends

1 ⭐ **What do you know?**

2 🎧 A:11 **Listen and read. Who lives at number 12?**

3 🎧 A:12 **Listen and say.**

1 dark hair
2 light hair
3 spiky hair
4 bald
5 handsome
6 beautiful
7 good-looking
8 cute

4 🎧 A:13 **Who's who in Activity 3? Listen and number.**

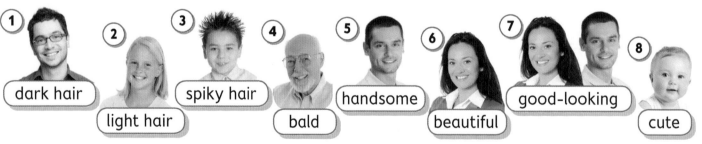

a brother ☐   **b** Jack ☐   **c** aunt ☐   **d** grandpa ☐

e uncle ☐   **f** sister ☐   **g** best friend ☐

Can identify words that describe what people look like

LOOK!

A:14

What **does** he/she **look like**?	**He's/She's** good-looking. He/She **has** straight, dark hair and brown eyes.
What **do** they **look like**?	**They're** tall and good-looking. They **have** short, light hair and blue eyes.
He/She **doesn't have** light hair.	They **don't have** light hair.

5 A:15 **Listen and read. Then look and say the names.**

1 She has light hair and blue eyes.
2 He has spiky hair and brown eyes.
3 She has straight hair and glasses.
4 He has brown hair and green eyes.
5 They have brown hair.

Maddy

Emma

Robbie

Dan

6 **Ask and answer. True or False?**

A: What does Maddy look like?
B: She has dark hair.
A: False! She has light hair.

7 **Ask and answer.**

A: Is it a person or an animal?
B: In this picture there's a person and an animal.
A: What do they look like?
B: They have curly, black hair.
A: Number 6!

> a beard   a mustache   bald
> beautiful   curly   fat   glasses
> good-looking   long   old   short
> spiky   straight   thin   ugly

 1

 **2**

3

4

 **5**

 **6**

 **7**

 **8**

9

10

11

12

Lesson 2

Can ask and answer about what someone looks like

13

8 🎧 A:16 Listen and say.

1. bossy
2. creative
3. sporty
4. lazy
5. smart
6. patient
7. talkative
8. helpful
9. friendly
10. hard-working

9 🎧 A:17/A:18 Listen to the song and write.

You have me, and I have you.
You talk, you listen, and I do, too.
We're friends. We're friends.

Ben's ¹_____ at home,
And he's ²_____ at school.
He's ³_____ and ⁴_____,
And very cool.
We're friends. We're friends.

Jim's sometimes ⁵_____,
But that's OK.
He's always ⁶_____ in every way.
We're friends. We're friends.
We're friends. We're friends.

10 Look at Activity 9 and write.

1 What's Ben like? _____

2 What's Jim like? _____

Can identify words that describe personality

11 A:20 **Listen and number. Then ask and answer.**

A:19

What's he/she like?	He's sporty and he's smart.
	She's bossy but hard-working.

I like him because he's patient.
I like her because she's friendly.

a   sporty but bossy

b   patient and funny

c   sporty and smart

d   smart but lazy

1
Dan

2
Emma

3
Maddy

4
Robbie

What's Maddy like?

She's smart but lazy.

12 **Circle.**

1   I like my new teacher (because / but) she isn't bossy.

2   He's sporty (and / but) smart. A perfect combination!

3   My best friend is talkative (and / but) funny. She makes me laugh!

4   She gets good grades (because / but) she's very hard-working.

5   He's lazy at home (but / and) he's hard-working in class. It's strange!

6   He has many friends (because / but) he's very friendly.

13 **Write a short message about two people in your family. Then share with a friend.**

_____

_____

_____

_____

I like my grandma because she isn't bossy. She's funny and creative.

15   Why do Polly and Mike think the skidoo has something to do with the missing diamonds? Discuss your answers.

Can understand a simple story / Can discuss a story

16 **Read the story again. Then write.**

1 Why do Polly and Mike have some ice cream? _____

2 Who is driving the skidoo? _____

3 Why does Polly say "Poor Gizmo"? _____

4 Do Mike and Polly know what the thieves look like? _____

5 Why is the driver of the skidoo in town? _____

6 Who does the driver of the skidoo work for? _____

17   **Role-play the story.**

18   **Read and write 1 to 5 (1 = not important, 5 = very important). Then compare with a friend.**

VALUES

Help your friends in class.

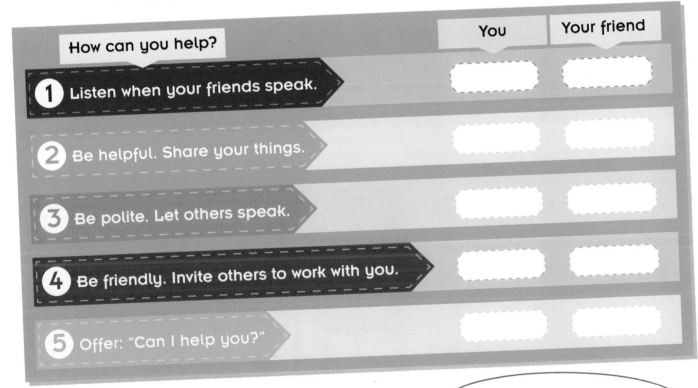

How can you help?	You	Your friend
1 Listen when your friends speak.		
2 Be helpful. Share your things.		
3 Be polite. Let others speak.		
4 Be friendly. Invite others to work with you.		
5 Offer: "Can I help you?"		

Be helpful. Share your things. 4.

Listen when your friends speak. 5.

HOME SCHOOL LINK Tell your family how you helped your friends in class today.

19 A:22 **Read. Is Seb happy?**

 **SKILLS**

The Torres family

Seb

From: seb@yoohoo.com
To: matt@gogomail.com
Subject: Spain!

Hi Matt,

I'm having a great summer here in Spain. I'm staying with the Torres family. They have a beautiful home in Madrid.

Carlos is 12. He's creative and very smart. He's patient, too. My Spanish isn't very good but he speaks great English! His grandma lives in Los Angeles and she speaks English with Carlos.

He has two sisters, Nerea and Lucia. Nerea is 18. She has beautiful, black hair, and she's very sporty. Lucia is nine. She's funny but she's very bossy. She wants to play games all the time!

See you soon,

Seb

20 **Circle T = True or F = False. Then correct the false sentences.**

1 Seb is in Madrid.   T / F
3 Carlos is creative and patient.   T / F
5 Nerea has long, light hair.   T / F

2 Carlos speaks Spanish with his grandma.   T / F
4 Seb's English isn't very good.   T / F
6 Lucia is funny but bossy.   T / F

21 **Write Seb's conversation with his mom. Then role-play with a friend.**

Are you having a good time?

I'm having a great time!

Seb's mom

Seb

1 Are you having a good time? _____
2 What's Carlos like? _____
3 What does he look like? _____
4 Does he have a brother or sister? _____
5 What are they like? _____

Can understand an email about what other people are like

22 **What do you know?**

23 **Look and read. Do you like the pictures? Why?**

A

This picture is by Auguste Renoir. It is in warm colors. Renoir was an artist from France. He lived from 1841 to 1919.

B

This picture is by Vincent van Gogh. It is in cool colors. Van Gogh was an artist from the Netherlands. He lived from 1853 to 1890.

24 **Look and say.**

It's Picture A!

1 This picture has a lot of yellow and red.
2 This picture has a lot of green and white.
3 This picture has cool colors.
4 This picture has warm colors.

MINI PROJECT

26 **Write about a painting.**

- **Think** of a painting you like. Who is the artist?

- **Plan** by making notes about where and when the artist lived. Are the colors in the painting warm or cool? How do they make you feel?

- **Write** five sentences about the painting.

- **Share** what you learned about the painting.

25 **Imagine and answer the questions. Then share with a friend.**

1 What time of day is it in Picture A?
2 How do the girls in Picture A feel?
3 How does Picture A make you feel?
4 How does Picture B make you feel?
5 How do you think van Gogh felt when he painted Picture B?

27 **Listen and number.**

28 **Circle. Then ask and answer.**

1   **A:** What does her sister look like? / What do they look like?
    B: They have straight hair and glasses.
2   **A:** What's he like? / What does he look like?
    B: He's creative and helpful. But he's lazy.
3   **A:** What's she like? / What does she look like?
    B: She has light hair but she doesn't have blue eyes. She has dark eyes!

29 **Write. Then ask and answer.**

1   What is your best friend like? _____
2   What does your mom look like? _____
3   Is your dad sporty and handsome? _____
4   Are you hard-working? _____
5   What do you look like? _____

I CAN

I can ask and answer about what someone looks like.
I can talk about what someone is like.
I can write about a painting.

30 **Create a new character.**

1 Circle.

My new character is...

thin fat ugly
handsome happy
beautiful bald
sporty
smart short
good-looking tall

2 Write.

My new character has... (thin, long, short, pink, etc.)

_____ _____ hair

a _____ body   _____ legs
a _____ head   _____ arms
a _____ face   _____ eyes
a _____ mouth   _____ ears

3 Draw. Then tell a friend.

4 Listen to your friend. Draw his/her new character.

5 Tell the class about your character. What is it like? What does it look like?

31 **I want to know more!**

My new character is tall and handsome. He has short, dark hair and green eyes. He's bossy but helpful. He likes rock climbing.

Now go to Poptropica
English World

Wider World 1
Families of the world

1 ⭐ **What do you know?**

2 🎧 A:25 **Listen and read. Are the families big or small?**

3 **Number the pictures.**

1 ● ○ ○ ○

Kyle's blog

In the United Kingdom, we have a lot of different families – some are big and some are small. My family is very big now. My mom has a new husband and he's great. He's very smart and he helps me with my homework. He has a son, too, so now I have a brother. We play soccer together every Saturday. We argue, but after five minutes, it's all OK! He's my brother and we're good friends.

Kyle, 12, United Kingdom

2 ● ○ ○ ○

Lang's blog

A lot of families here in China have only one child. My friends and I don't have brothers or sisters but we aren't sad. Brothers and sisters can be bossy! We can do what we want. We have a good life and we have very good friends. I live with my mom and dad, and my grandma and grandpa. It's fun because my grandparents play games with me. I love my small family.

Lang, 11, China

Can understand texts about families around the world

James's blog

I live in the United States. Our house is big. We have a very big kitchen and there are four bathrooms in the house. We have three washing machines for all the dirty clothes. My friends have small families but I have a mom and dad, three sisters, and three brothers. Big families are great! In my family, the big children help the small children. My sister, Jill, is 17 and she helps me with my homework and music practice. She's bossy but she's nice, too.

James, 12, United States

5 Ask and answer.

1 How big is your family?
2 Are families in your country big or small?

4 Find the words. Then match.

1	argue	**a**	doing something again and again to get better at it
2	washing machine	**b**	to not agree when talking to someone
3	practice	**c**	you use this to wash clothes

YOUR TURN!

What is good and bad about big and small families? Discuss in pairs. Then tell the class.

	Good	Bad
Small family	more time with parents	no brothers or sisters to play with
Big family		

2 My life

1 **What do you know?**

2 A:26 **Listen and read. Who is hard-working? Who is lazy?**

1 After school, Maddy meets her friends.

Go away, Kipper!

2 In the afternoon, Emma and Dan do their homework. Maddy and Robbie play video games.

You should do your homework first.

I know. Go away, Kipper!

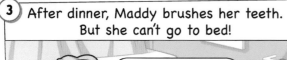

3 After dinner, Maddy brushes her teeth. But she can't go to bed!

Go away, Kipper!

4 You must do your homework now.

5 Before bed, Maddy does her homework.

Your Pet
How long is his tail?

Oh, no. My homework is about Kipper! Kipper, where are you?

3 A:27 **Listen and say.**

1 brush my teeth

2 make my bed

3 wash my face

4 clean my room

5 do my homework

6 meet my friends

7 study before a test

8 take notes in class

9 take out the trash

10 be on time

4 A:28 **Work with a friend. Listen and play the memory game.**

Can identify daily activities and routines

5 A:30 **Listen and number. Then say. What must Emma do before bed?**

A:29 **LOOK!**

| You **must brush** your teeth. | (Order) |
| You **should brush** your teeth. | (Advice) |

a

b

c

d

She must take out the trash.

---

6 **Unscramble and write. Circle A = advice or O = order. Then say.**

1 wash / you / face / bed / must / your / before
   _____   A / O

2 teeth / after meals / you / brush / should / your
   _____   A / O

3 room / should / clean / you / your / every day
   _____   A / O

4 homework / your / must / you / do / now
   _____   A / O

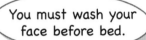
You must wash your face before bed.

---

7 **Look and match. Then say. What advice can you give Maddy?**

1
Sorry, I'm late.

2
I have a test on Monday.

3
I'm bored.

4
I don't have class notes.

a take notes in class

b meet her friends

c be on time

d study before a test

She should be on time.

8 A:31 **Listen and say. Then number.**

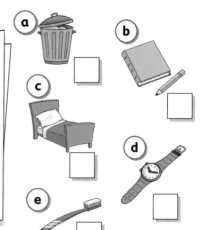

	Monday	Tuesday	Wednesday	Thursday	Friday
1 always					
2 usually					
3 often					
4 sometimes					
5 never					

9 A:32/ A:33 **Listen to the song and write.**

SONG

I ¹ _____ wash my face before school.
But I ² _____ brush my hair so I look cool.
I ³ _____ make my bed
And I ⁴ _____ help my mom.
But I never, never clean my room.
I never, never clean my room.

My brother ⁵ _____ his room.
My sister cleans her room.
My friends clean their rooms,
But not me! Oh, no! Not me!
I never, never clean my room.
I never, never clean my room.

Where's my sister's kite? Is it under the bed?
And on the chair what's that? A monster's head!
My brother's ball is here, too.
But where is it? Well, I don't know
Because I never, never clean my room.
I never, never clean my room.
Never, never clean my room.

10 **Look at Activity 9 and write.**

1 He _____ makes his bed.
2 He _____ washes his face before school.
3 He _____ brushes his hair.
4 He _____ cleans his room.

Can use always, usually, often, sometimes, never

11   **Look at the chart and say.**

She always brushes her teeth.

I **always brush** my teeth.
He **usually brushes** his teeth.
She **often brushes** her teeth.
They **sometimes brush** their teeth.
We **never brush** our teeth.

Sasha's week	Monday	Tuesday	Wednesday	Thursday	Friday
brushes her teeth					
makes her bed					
does her homework					
meets her friends					
cleans her room					

12 **Check (✓) to complete the chart about yourself. Then write and say.**

My week	Monday	Tuesday	Wednesday	Thursday	Friday
brush my teeth					
make my bed					
do my homework					
clean my room					
take out the trash					

1 _____
2 _____
3 _____
4 _____
5 _____

I sometimes take out the trash.

14   Why are Polly and Mike excited to find red ribbons in Smith's shopping bag? Discuss your answers.

15 **Read the story again and circle T = True or F = False. Then correct the false sentences.**

1	Smith is working out at the training camp.	T / F
2	The igloo is made of fire.	T / F
3	The fire makes Polly and Mike sleepy.	T / F
4	Mike and Polly don't see Smith leave because of the snow.	T / F
5	Smith leaves his skidoo at the training camp.	T / F
6	The new red ribbons are for Hector Frost's dog.	T / F

16 **Role-play the story.**

17 **What do you give to friends and family? Write *never*, *sometimes*, *often*, *usually*, or *always*. Then share with a friend.**

VALUES

Giving is great.

What do you do?	You	Your friend
1 Give birthday cards.		
2 Give small birthday presents.		
3 Share music.		
4 Send text messages.		
5 Give tickets for a show.		
6 Invite friends to play.		

Do you give birthday cards?

Yes, I always give birthday cards.

HOME SCHOOL LINK Make a card to give to someone in your family.

18 A:36 **Read and circle. What is Peter's score?**

 SKILLS

QUIZ! ARE YOU A M RNING PERSON?

Some people like mornings. What about you?

1 Do you get up on time in the morning?

1 No, never.
2 Yes, sometimes.
3 Yes, often.
4 Yes, usually.
5 Yes, always.

2 Do you have a big breakfast?

1 No, never.
2 Yes, sometimes.
3 Yes, often.
4 Yes, usually.
5 Yes, always.

3 Do you talk to your friends and family before school?

1 No, never.
2 Yes, sometimes.
3 Yes, often.
4 Yes, usually.
5 Yes, always.

4 Do you make your bed in the morning?

1 No, never.
2 Yes, sometimes.
3 Yes, often.
4 Yes, usually.
5 Yes, always.

5 Do you make your family's breakfast?

1 No, never.
2 Yes, sometimes.
3 Yes, often.
4 Yes, usually.
5 Yes, always.

6 Do you get to school on time?

1 No, never.
2 Yes, sometimes.
3 Yes, often.
4 Yes, usually.
5 Yes, always.

YOUR SCORE!

6–14 You're not a morning person. You shouldn't do important things before lunch!

15–22 You're OK in the morning but not great.

23–30 Wow, you're a morning person. You should do everything in the morning!

19 **Look at Activity 18 and talk about Peter's day. Then quiz your partner. Is he/she a morning person?**

> I always get up on time in the morning.

TIP!

should + not = shouldn't

  20 A:37 **Listen and circle.**

1 Emma (is / isn't) a morning person.
2 Emma (always / sometimes) makes her bed in the morning.
3 Emma (sometimes / never) has a small breakfast.
4 Emma (never / often) helps in the kitchen in the morning.
5 Emma (likes / doesn't like) talking in the morning.
6 Emma (often / always) gets to school on time.

Can assess whether someone is a morning person

21 **What do you know?**

22 **A:38** **Read. Is Jonas healthy?**

Jonas is a soccer player. He must practice every day and he often meets his friends for a game of tennis, too. His energy comes from his food. Pasta is his favorite! He's very healthy because he eats meat, vegetables, cereal, and fruit. His bones and teeth are strong because he likes drinking milk. Jonas always brushes his teeth after meals and again before bed, and he always goes to the dentist for a check-up in March and September.

What kinds of foods are bad for your teeth? Why?

HEALTHY MENU FOR TUESDAY

★ BREAKFAST ★
Cereal with milk
Toast
A banana
Orange juice

LUNCH
Chicken pasta with green salad
An orange
Water

DINNER
Vegetable soup and bread
Fish, potatoes, and carrots
Apple pie
Milk

23 **Say.**

1. Jonas likes playing soccer and...
2. Jonas's favorite food is...
3. After meals, he always...
4. Jonas likes drinking...

24 **Write.**

1. Apples and oranges are examples of this. _____
2. This is a white drink. It makes bones and teeth strong. _____
3. This is a drink made from fruit. _____
4. To keep your teeth healthy, you should sometimes visit this place. _____
5. This is an orange vegetable. _____

MINI PROJECT

25 **Make a menu.**

- **Think** about what foods are healthy and what foods are bad for your teeth.

- **Plan** a menu with three healthy meals for breakfast, lunch, and dinner. Include main meals, drinks, and desserts.

- **Write** your menu.

- **Share** your menu with your friends and try it at home.

26 **A:39** Listen and check (✓).

1 a b

2 a b

3 a b

4 a b

27 **A:40** Listen and circle.

1 Her train never comes (on time / late).
2 He (usually / often) goes to bed late.
3 Tomorrow, the students (must / should) give the mini-project to the teacher.
4 He (shouldn't / doesn't) eat chocolate every day and he (never / should) go see a dentist.

28 Unscramble and write. Then number.

a likes / time / be / she / on / to

_____

b trash / the / I / out / always / take

_____

c go / late / to / you / bed / shouldn't

_____

d clean / room / should / your / you

_____

e often / friends / I / meet / my

_____

1 I'm seeing them this afternoon.

2 She's never late.

3 I like helping at home.

4 It's so dirty!

5 You need lots of sleep.

I CAN

I can give orders and advice using *you must* and *you should*.
I can talk about how often I do things.
I can create a healthy menu.

Sue

Alex

Alice

Max

1 Choose a person. What is he/she like?

2 Is he/she healthy?

3 What does he/she eat for breakfast?

4 Write about his/her week.

(Sue / Alex / Alice / Max) always _____ .

He/She usually _____ .

_____ often _____ .

_____ sometimes _____ .

_____ never _____ .

5 Find someone who chose the same person. Compare.

Alex is patient and hard-working. He eats two eggs with toast and fruit for breakfast. He always brushes his teeth after eating.

I think Alex is creative and sporty. He has coffee, yogurt, and an apple for breakfast. He is never late for work.

30 **I want to know more!**

Now go to Poptropica English World

Review Units 1 and 2

1 Read, look, and number.

1 My brother is seven. He has curly, brown hair and gray eyes. He's very funny but he's lazy.

2 My mom has long, light hair and blue eyes. She's sporty. She plays tennis every day. She's talkative and sometimes bossy.

Amy

3 My teacher isn't very tall. She has long, straight hair. She's a good teacher because she's smart and always very patient.

4 My friend is in my class at school. He's short and has light hair and glasses.

a Fergus

b Mrs. Taylor

c Ben

d Mrs. Picton

2 Ask and answer.

A: What does Amy's teacher look like?
A: What's Amy's teacher like?

B: She has long, straight hair.
B: She's smart and patient.

3 Ask and answer.

1 What must you do in the morning?
2 What should you do after school?
3 What must you do before bed?
4 What should you do every day?

I must make my bed in the morning.

Can talk about physical appearance and personality

4 **A:41** **Read and say. Then listen and check your answers.**

my   his   her   our   their

In the evening,...

1   I sometimes   (meet/friends)
2   Fergus and Ben always   (do/homework)
3   Fergus never   (clean/room)
4   Mom often   (wash/hair)
5   I usually   (make/bed)
6   Ben and I always   (brush/teeth)

> In the evening, I sometimes meet my friends.

5 **Write three sentences.**

> My dad never takes out the trash and he never sets the table for dinner.

1 _____

2 _____

3 _____

I   mom/dad
sister/brother
he   she   they

always
sometimes
never

but

do my homework
clean the bathroom
take out the trash

and

set the table for dinner
go to bed before me
get dressed before breakfast

3 Free time

1 ⭐ **What do you know?**

2 🎧 A:42 **Listen and read. Is Robbie good at throwing?**

1 Hey, Emma. Let's play soccer!

I like reading comic books. I don't like playing soccer, Robbie.

2 Ok, then... Hey, Emma! Catch!

You're good at kicking balls, Robbie, but you aren't good at throwing them!

3 I am good at throwing! Look!

4 Oh, no!

Are you good at climbing trees, Robbie? Ha, ha!

3 🎧 A:43 **Listen and say.**

1. hitting
2. kicking
3. throwing
4. catching
5. diving
6. going shopping
7. telling jokes
8. reading poetry
9. jumping on the trampoline

4 🎧 A:44 **Listen and number using the words in Activity 3.**

a ☐ b ☐ c ☐ d ☐ e ☐ f ☐ g ☐ h ☐ i ☐

Can talk about free-time activities

LOOK!

What **am I** good at?	**I'm** good at hitting.
What's **he**/**she** good at?	**He's**/**She's** good at hitting.
What **are they** good at?	**They're** good at hitting.
He/**She isn't** good at catching. / **They aren't** good at catching.	
What **does he**/**she like**/**love** doing?	**He**/**She likes**/**loves** going shopping.

5 A:46 **Listen and number.**

Number 1. What's she good at?

She's good at diving.

6 **Look at Activity 5. Ask and answer.**

7 A:47 **Listen and match. Then say.**

1 playing video games

2 in-line skating

3 playing chess

4 playing the drums

5 acting

6 singing karaoke

7 running races

8 singing in a choir

8 A:48/ A:49 **Listen to the song and write.**

SONG

Chorus:
Come and have fun at the Fun Club! Come here and meet new friends.
¹ _____, drawing pictures, ² _____.
At the Fun Club, the fun never ends.
What do you like doing?
Do you like playing the ³ _____, or ⁴ _____?
There's fun for everyone.
What are you good at? Are you good at playing ⁵ _____?
We love Fun Club. It's fun here! Yes! Yes! Yes!

(Chorus)

9 **Ask and answer.**

A: What are you good at?
B: I'm good at telling jokes.
A: What do you like doing?
B: I love jumping on the trampoline but I don't like running races.

Can identify more free-time activities and hobbies

LOOK!

A:50

What were you doing yesterday at 7:00?	I was drawing pictures.
What was he/she doing yesterday at 7:00?	He/She was drawing pictures.
What were they doing yesterday at 7:00?	They were drawing pictures.
Were you drawing pictures?	Yes, I was. / No, I wasn't.
Was he/she drawing pictures?	Yes, he/she was. / No, he/she wasn't.
Were they drawing pictures?	Yes, they were. / No, they weren't.

10 A:51 **Listen and circle. Then ask and answer.**

p.m.	Robbie	Emma	Maddy and Dan
2:45	studying English	playing volleyball	reading in the classroom
	singing in music class	jumping on the trampoline	drawing pictures
5:00	playing chess at school	shopping	doing their homework
	reading comic books	playing video games	acting

What was Robbie doing yesterday at 2:45?

He was studying English.

11 A:52 **Listen and match. Then ask and answer.**

11:00 reading in class

10:00 in-line skating

12:00 having lunch

7:00 walking to school

7:00 sleeping

11:00 playing chess

7:00 having breakfast

1

2

3

What was Robbie doing yesterday at 7:00?

10:00 swimming

10:00 writing a story

He was...

13 Are the tracks that Polly and Mike see really wolf tracks? Discuss your answers.

Can understand a simple story / Can discuss a story

14 **Read the story again. Then circle.**

1 The skidoo woke (Mike / Polly / Polly's mom) up at (1:00 a.m. / 2:00 a.m. / 12:00 a.m.) on (Tuesday / Thursday / Saturday).

2 The (skidoo / wolf) was going towards (town / the mountains / the training camp) early on Thursday morning.

3 Mike and Polly are eating (breakfast / lunch / dinner) at (Mike's / Polly's) house.

4 (Hector / Mike / Polly's mom) plays soccer on (Mondays / Fridays / Saturdays).

5 (Smith / Mike / Polly) is good at (soccer / chess / acting) and (running races / making fires / finding thieves).

6 The (red / pink / orange) ribbon fell off (Gizmo / the skidoo / a wolf).

15 **Role-play the story.**

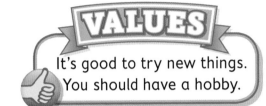

VALUES

It's good to try new things.
You should have a hobby.

16 **Check (✓) what you want to try.**

1 You're good at sports. You should...

take dance lessons.

join a sports team.

learn martial arts.

2 You're good at drawing and painting. You should...

take an art class.

learn to draw comic strips.

learn to make jewelry.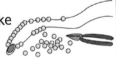

3 You're good at singing and acting. You should...

learn to play an instrument.

join the school drama club.

start a band with friends.

4 You're good at technology. You should...

learn computer programming.

learn to make video games.

build a website.

I'm good at technology.

You should learn computer programming.

 Try a new activity with your family.

17 Read and match.

Laura   Antonio   Fred

SPORTS CAMP

Do YOU like doing sports?

9:30	soccer
10:30	swimming and diving
11:30	jumping on the trampoline
12:30	basketball
2:00	tennis

Evening fun!

THEATER CAMP

Do YOU want to be a star?

At Theater Camp you can:

make costumes   sing

dance   act

There's a fantastic show every Friday!

18 Listen again. Then write.

catching and hitting balls   playing basketball   running and diving
singing and acting   singing and dancing   throwing and catching

1 Laura is good at _____ .
2 Laura isn't good at _____ .
3 Antonio loves _____ .
4 Antonio isn't very good at _____ .
5 Fred likes _____ .
6 Fred isn't good at _____ .

19 Look and choose. Tell a friend.

I like Sports Camp because I love diving and I'm good at playing tennis.

20 **What do you know?**

21 **Read. Then write T = True or F = False.**
A:56

This is Harry Gregson-Williams. He writes music for movies and video games.

What movies is your music in?
The *Shrek* movies, the *Narnia* movies, and a lot of others.

You write music for video games, too. Do you like playing video games?
Video games are OK but they aren't my favorite thing. I write my music on computers so I don't like playing on computers when I'm at home.

What instruments can you play?
I'm good at playing the piano and I can play the drums. I'm good at singing, too.

What's your favorite music?
Oh... I can't answer that question. I love listening to violins and trumpets but I love a lot of music!

1 He's good at playing the piano. _____
2 He can't sing. _____
3 He likes violin music. _____
4 He writes the stories for movies. _____
5 He loves playing video games. _____

22 **Correct the false sentences in Activity 21. Say.**

23 **Listen to the music and number.**
A:57

violins ☐

drums ☐

piano ☐

trumpet ☐

MINI PROJECT

24 **Write interview questions.**

- **Think** Do you know any musical people like Harry Gregson-Williams?

- **Plan** Choose one musical person and the things you want to know about him/her.

- **Write** Create five questions for a "Discover a great musician" interview. Are good interview questions short or long, polite or rude? Check your questions.

- **Share** Present your interview to the class with a friend.

What were they doing yesterday?

1 Emma	2 Dan	3 Maddy	4 Mom and Dad
a ☐	a ☐	a ☐	a ☐
b ☐	b ☐	b ☐	b ☐

26 **Unscramble and write questions. Then write the answers.**

Shopping

1 Emma / playing / was / chess

_____

2 the / drums / was / playing / Emma

_____

3 were / shopping / Mom / and / Dad

_____

4 comic / Mom / were / and / reading / Dad / books

_____

27 **Think of an activity each person or pair did yesterday. Write it down. Then ask and answer.**

You	Your mom/dad	Your friend	Your brother/sister

Was Tom in-line skating yesterday?   No, he wasn't. Guess again!

I CAN

I can talk about what people are good at and not good at doing.   ☐ ☐ ☐

I can talk about what people were doing yesterday at different times.   ☐ ☐ ☐

I can write interview questions for a musical person.   ☐ ☐ ☐

28 Follow the lines. Find and unscramble the letters. Then write.

good at   loves   likes

1 Robbie _____is good at acting_____. He _____, too.
2 Maddy _____. She _____ playing
_____, too.
3 Dan _____. He _____, too.
4 Emma _____. She _____, too.

29 **What new things should they try? Give advice in pairs.**

Robbie, you like acting. You should try singing, too.

30 **I want to know more!**

Now go to Poptropica English World

Lesson 10

Can use what I have learned in Unit 3

Wider World 2
Funny sports

1 ⭐ **What do you know?**

2 🎧 A:59 **Listen and read. What are the people doing?**

3 💬 **Look and say.**

1 This is a ball sport.
2 This is a sport with food.
3 This is a winter sport.
4 People ride in this sport.
5 People run in this sport.

> It's elephant polo!

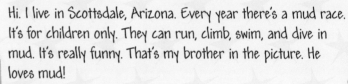

1

Mud racing

Hi. I live in Scottsdale, Arizona. Every year there's a mud race. It's for children only. They can run, climb, swim, and dive in mud. It's really funny. That's my brother in the picture. He loves mud!

Bianca, 11, United States

2

Cheese rolling

Every May, people roll a big cheese wheel down Cooper's Hill. Then everyone runs to catch the cheese. The winner can eat it! My dad likes doing the race but he never wins. He isn't very good at running!

Freddy, 11, United Kingdom

Can understand texts about funny sports

3

Reindeer racing

People love doing this sport in winter here in Tromso. The people don't ride the reindeer. They go on skis. The races are in the streets of the town and everyone shouts for their favorite reindeer. I love watching reindeer racing.

Ingrid, 11, Norway

4

Elephant polo

People usually play polo on horses but, here in Jaipur, people sometimes play polo on elephants. They hit the ball with very long sticks. I don't play because I'm not good at hitting the ball. But I like watching.

Rajeev, 12, India

4 **Read again and choose. Tell a friend.**

A: I want to do cheese rolling.
B: Why?
A: Because I'm good at running and I love eating cheese!

YOUR TURN!

- **Does your country have any unusual or funny sports? Discuss in pairs.**
- **Tell the class.**

5 Write.

In our country, people love...

4 Around the world

1 **What do you know?**

2 **Listen and read. Does Dan like crocodiles?**

ROUND-THE-WORLD Holiday

COMPETITION

Dan: Look! There's a competition for a round-the-world trip. The winner goes to the United Kingdom, Egypt, and China, then Australia and Brazil.

Maddy: Wow, there are a lot of interesting places you can see in the United Kingdom. In Egypt there are the Pyramids, and in China there's the Great Wall.

Dan: Sounds great! And in Brazil and Australia there are some beautiful beaches.

Maddy: But, mmm, Dan... there are crocodiles, sharks, and big spiders in Australia, too.

Dan: What?!

Maddy: Don't worry. There are a lot of children in this competition. There's little chance of winning!

3 **Listen and say.**

1  China
2 Korea
3 Japan
4 Australia
5  the United States

6  Mexico
7  Colombia
8 Brazil
9 Argentina
10  the United Kingdom

11 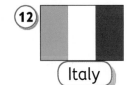 Spain
12  Italy
13 Egypt
14 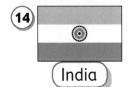 India

4 **Which continent is your country in?**

Africa   Asia   Australia   Europe
North America   South America

Can identify countries and continents

5 **B:05 Listen and ✓ (= There are) or ✗ (= There aren't). Then say.**

LOOK!

B:04

There's a rain forest in Brazil.

There isn't a rain forest in Korea.

There are some penguins in Argentina.

There aren't any penguins in Italy.

WILD VACATIONS

See these beautiful animals in the wild!

	penguins	monkeys	snakes
Argentina	✓		
Italy	✗		
China			

> There are some penguins in Argentina.

6 **Play the game.**

A: There aren't any penguins. There aren't any monkeys. There are some snakes.
B: It's Italy!

7 **Look and say.**

> boat   dog   monkey   people   rocks   shark
> in the ocean   in the tree   on the beach

> There's a dog on the beach. There aren't any people in the tree.

8 B:06 **Listen and number. Then say.**

a **pyramid** ☐

b **statue** ☐

c **cave** ☐

d **volcano** ☐

e **city** ☐

f **town** ☐

g **farm** ☐

h **factory** ☐

i **castle** ☐

TIP!
factories
cities
volcanoes

9 B:07/ B:08 **Listen to the song and write.**

SONG

Chorus:
The drums are calling.
My home is calling.
I want to be there – in ¹_____ !
Tell me about your country!
I can tell you a lot.
Is there a ²_____ ?
Yes, there is. It's hot, hot, hot!
(Chorus)

Are there any ³_____ ?
Yes, there are… and there are
lakes, ⁴_____ , forests, and
mountains.
It's a beautiful place!
(Chorus)
Are there any old ⁵_____ ?
Yes, there are. It's true.
With wonderful big ⁶_____ ,
And ⁷_____ , too.
(Chorus)

10 **Look at Activity 9. Ask and answer.**

What things are there in Mexico?

There's a desert in Mexico.

Can identify and talk about places of interest

LOOK!

B:09

Is there a pyramid in the city?	Yes, there is. / No, there isn't.
Are there any beaches in Australia?	Yes, there are some beautiful beaches in Australia.
Are there any volcanoes in the United Kingdom?	No, there aren't.

11 B:10 **Listen and number. Then ask and answer.**

a

b

c

d

e

Is there a volcano in the city?

No, there isn't.

12 Ask and answer about your country.

A: Are there any deserts?
B: No, there aren't.

14 Do the children want the diamonds? Why does Frost think that they want them? Discuss your answers.

15 Read the story again. Then write

1 What goes north of Mike and Polly?

_____

2 Which two people live at Bollington Hall?

_____

3 What do Mike and Polly suspect?

_____

4 What does Frost want Smith to do?

_____

5 Why does Frost want Mike and Polly to go away?

_____

16 Role-play the story.

VALUES

Teamwork is important.

17 Check (✓) the pictures where people work on a team.

① ☐

② ☐

③ ☐

④ ☐

18 Write three things that can only be done on a team. Tell the class.

1 _____

2 _____

3 _____

Tell your family why teamwork is important.

19   B:12   **Read. What is the name of the statue?**

Dear Archie,

Hello from Egypt! It's very hot here but it's fun. This postcard is from Giza. In the desert at Giza, there are some big pyramids and there's a big statue, too. It's called the Sphinx. It has a man's head and a lion's body. It's very, very old. From Giza, you can see the city of Cairo.

Our hotel is on an island in the River Nile. There aren't any cars on the island. Everyone goes by boat. I can see some big white birds in the river. This round-the-world trip is fantastic! Are there any fun lessons at school this week?

See you soon!

Mia

Archie Joseph
103 Park Street
Denver, CO 80216
United States

20 B:13   **Listen and underline on the postcard. Then write.**

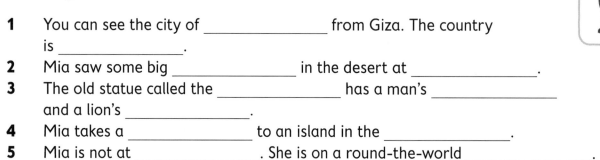

1 You can see the city of _____ from Giza. The country is _____.

2 Mia saw some big _____ in the desert at _____.

3 The old statue called the _____ has a man's _____ and a lion's _____.

4 Mia takes a _____ to an island in the _____.

5 Mia is not at _____. She is on a round-the-world _____.

21   **Where should Mia travel in your country? Discuss with a partner.**

A: Mia can go to Whitesea Island.
B: Why?
A: Because there are some good beaches and there's a pretty waterfall, too.
B: OK. Let's choose Whitesea Island.

22 **What do you know?**

23   **Read. Does Inuk like the summer or the winter?**

i-Blog

Home | My favorites | Pictures | Log out

My recent pictures

Click here to read more

My recent posts

Hi. I'm Inuk. I live in Greenland. Winter and summer are very different here.

Winter

In the winter, we don't see the sun very much. There's one long night for four weeks in December and January. There are some big snowstorms and it's very, very cold. We go to school by skidoo because we can't use a car.

Summer

In the summer, there aren't any snowstorms. There are often long, sunny days. For a month, it's never nighttime! I go kayaking and fishing every day. The summer is great but it's very short. In September, it's time for my winter clothes again.

---

24 **Read again and say *summer* or *winter*.**

1 People use boats.
2 People use skidoos.
3 There are very long days.
4 There are big snowstorms.
5 There isn't very much sun.

25 **Choose a place you want to live and tell a friend.**

A: I want to live in Greenland because I love playing in the snow.
B: I don't want to live there. I love the sun.

MINI PROJECT

26 **Write a blog post.**

• **Think** about summer and winter in your country. Are they very different? What months are summer and winter?

• **Plan** by making a note of three things you like and three things you don't like about each season.

• **Write** a blog post. Include what summer and winter are like where you live, what you like and don't like about them, what clothes you wear, how you get to school, and what you do in each season.

• **Share** your blog with the class.

---

27 B:15 Listen and check (✓).

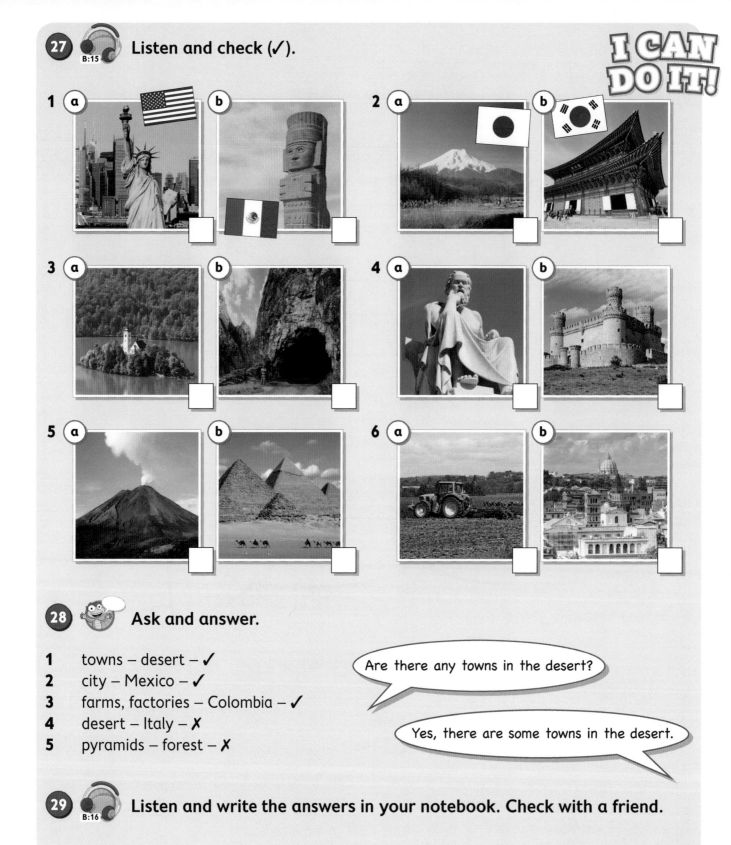

1 a ☐ b ☐   **2** a ☐ b ☐

3 a ☐ b ☐   **4** a ☐ b ☐

5 a ☐ b ☐   **6** a ☐ b ☐

28 Ask and answer.

1 towns – desert – ✓
2 city – Mexico – ✓
3 farms, factories – Colombia – ✓
4 desert – Italy – ✗
5 pyramids – forest – ✗

Are there any towns in the desert?

Yes, there are some towns in the desert.

29 B:16 Listen and write the answers in your notebook. Check with a friend.

I CAN

I can talk about places using *There is/isn't* and *There are/aren't*. ☐ ☐ ☐
I can ask and answer about places using *Is there a…* and *Are there any…* ? ☐ ☐ ☐
I can write a blog post about seasons in my country. ☐ ☐ ☐

30 Look at the pictures and circle the words in the puzzle.

M	C	D	E	S	E	R	T	X	C	A	V	E	K
E	M	W	V	T	V	G	Q	N	O	L	P	E	W
X	B	N	F	A	R	M	M	J	L	Y	T	B	R
I	V	C	X	T	Z	G	X	K	O	R	E	A	Z
C	M	S	D	U	F	G	H	J	M	K	L	Q	C
O	X	C	V	E	B	P	Y	T	B	R	C	W	H
N	J	M	S	D	F	G	H	J	I	K	I	L	I
Q	A	U	S	T	R	A	L	I	A	W	T	R	N
T	P	Y	P	Z	X	C	V	B	N	M	Y	S	A
D	A	F	V	O	L	C	A	N	O	G	H	J	K
Z	N	C	V	B	N	M	Q	W	R	T	Y	P	L

31 Unscramble the words and find the secret message.

1 There are pyramids and deserts.

EXOMCI

☐☐☐☐☐☐
     6

2 There's a very large rain forest.

RIZBAL

☐☐☐☐☐☐
11 9 12 1

3 There are pandas and snakes.

NAICH

☐☐☐☐☐
  8

4 There are beaches but there aren't any pyramids.

AASUTRIAL

☐☐☐☐☐☐☐☐☐
  4 10

5 There's a very long river.

TEYGP

☐☐☐☐☐
2 5 13

6 There are castles and farms but there aren't any deserts.

TEH NEUDIT

☐☐☐☐☐☐☐☐☐
     3

NIGDKMO

☐☐☐☐☐☐☐
   7

Secret Message = ☐☐☐ , ☐☐☐☐☐☐☐☐☐☐ !
1 2 3 4 5 6 7 8 9 10 11 12 13

32 I want to know more!

Now go to Poptropica English World

Lesson 10

Review Units 3 and 4

1 Read. Then write.

answering   good at   helping
like   sunny   watching

Hi, again. Do you remember me? I'm Amy. Last weekend, I was [1] _____ at my school's Open Day. I was showing people the school and [2] _____ their questions. I [3] _____ doing this type of thing.

I'm Amy's teacher. Last weekend was good weather. It was [4] _____. I was [5] _____ Amy and the other students. They were [6] _____ their jobs. I love seeing my students helping the school.

2 B:17 Listen and write.

What was Amy's mom doing?

_____

Is she good at it? _____
Does she like it? _____

What was Amy's brother doing?

_____

What does he like doing? _____
Is he good at it? _____

What was Amy's friend doing?

_____

Does he love doing it? _____
Is he good at it? _____

Can talk about free-time activities and hobbies

3 Write the country name.

1 The flag of this country is yellow, blue, and red.   _____
2 This country is in Europe. It has a red and yellow flag.   _____
3 In this big Asian country there are many big cities and
  there is a very long wall.   _____
4 This country is an island. It has a red and white flag.   _____
5 There are many mountains and volcanoes in this country.
  It's next to the United States.   _____
6 There are many large lakes in this big country in South America.
  It has a blue, white, and yellow flag. It's next to Brazil. _____

4 Think about your town or city. Check (✓) the true sentences. Then ask and answer.

1 There are some lakes.   ☐

2 There are some beaches.   ☐

3 There are some farms.   ☐

4 There is a volcano.   ☐

5 There are some caves.   ☐

6 There are some factories.   ☐

> Are there any lakes?

> Yes, there are.

5 Write about your country.

In my country there are _____
_____
_____
_____
_____
_____
_____
_____
_____
_____
_____

5 Shopping

1 ⭐ **What do you know?**

2 🎧 B:18 **Listen and read. Does Emma buy the jacket?**

1
How much is that scarf?
It's six dollars and fifty cents.

2
And how much are those sunglasses?
They're fifteen dollars.

3
Wow! I love that jacket, and it's only twelve dollars.

4
May I buy the jacket, please?
$124.00
Yes, of course. One hundred and twenty-four dollars, please.
What?!

3 🎧 B:19 **Listen and say.**

1. jacket
2. swimsuit
3. watch
4. bracelet
5. wallet
6. handbag
7. umbrella
8. gloves
9. sunglasses

I like that blue jacket.

4 **Look and say. Use words from Activity 3.**

LOOK!
B:20

| How much is this/that jacket? | It's ninety dollars and fifty cents. |
| How much are these/those sunglasses? | They're thirty dollars. |

5 B:21 **Listen and write. Then ask and answer.**

1. $_____
2. $_____
3. $_____
4. $_____
5. $_____
6. $_____
7. $_____
8. $_____
9. $_____

How much is that handbag?

It's fifty-nine dollars and fifty cents.

6 **Look and imagine prices. Then role-play the conversation.**

A: How much is that pen?
B: It's three dollars and fifty cents.
A: May I buy it, please?

1. pen
2. candy
3. guitar
4. drum set
5. computer
6. T-shirt
7. scarf
8. sandals

7 **Listen and number. Then say.**

 B:22

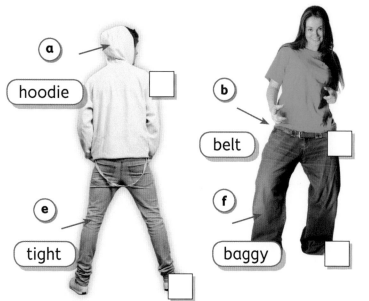

(a) hoodie ☐

(b) belt ☐

(e) tight ☐

(f) baggy ☐

(c)  cheap ☐

(d)  expensive ☐

(g)  old-fashioned ☐

(h)  modern ☐

VOCABULARY

8 **Listen to the song and write.**

B:23/ B:24

SONG

TIP!

That jacket is **too** tight.

Those sunglasses are **too** expensive.

9 **Look and say.**

jacket/tight
pants/short
scarf/long
socks/baggy
sunglasses/big

Her sunglasses are too big.

That jacket's too ¹ _____ .
And the color's too ² _____ .
That hat's too ³ _____ .
And the size isn't right.
Chorus:
I only like wearing…
Baggy pants, baggy pants,
baggy pants, baggy pants.
Baggy pants are ⁴ _____ ,
baggy pants are cool.
Baggy pants rule!
That sweatshirt's too ⁵ _____ .
Those shorts are too ⁶ _____ .
Those gloves are too ⁷ _____ .
And the color is wrong.
(Chorus)

Can identify words that describe clothing and accessories

10 Listen and match.
Then ask and answer.

①

②

③

④

ⓐ

ⓑ

ⓒ

ⓓ

> Whose sunglasses are these?

> They're not mine. They're...

11 Look at Activity 10 and write.

1 The jacket is _____ Dan's _____. It's _____ Dan's _____ jacket. It's _____ his _____.
2 The sunglasses are _____. They're _____ sunglasses.
They're _____.
3 The bracelet _____.
_____
4 The swimsuit _____.
_____

13 **Why does Smith push Polly into the water? Discuss your answers.**

14 **Read the story again. Then circle.**

1 (Mike / An explorer / Smith) is buying a jacket from Polly's mom.
2 The jacket is (500 Frost dollars / 550 Ice dollars / 500 Ice dollars).
3 The explorers want to go to (the Ice Palace / the lake / Bollington Hall).
4 (The explorers / Polly and Mike / Smith and Hector Frost) made a hole in the ice.
5 Gizmo (saves Polly / digs a hole in the ice / chases Smith).
6 Smith works for (the explorers / Frost, Inc. / the police).

15 **Role-play the story.**

16 **Look and match. Then discuss with a friend. Compare your choices.**

VALUES

Dress correctly for each occasion.

A lunchtime beach party in the summer. **1**

Dinner with older family members. **2**

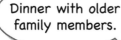

School graduation ceremony. **3**

a
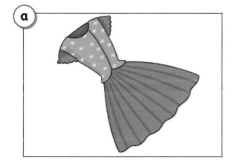

b

c

d

e

f

Plan an outfit for an event that you are going to.

Lesson 6

Can understand details of a story / Can talk about dressing correctly for different occasions

17   B:28 **Read. Are these stories, ads, or emails?**

CRAZY CLOTHING™ Are your clothes too small, too old, or too boring?

COME TO **CRAZY CLOTHING**

We have a lot of clothes for boys and girls. Beach clothes, sports clothes, school clothes. They're all here at CRAZY CLOTHING!

24 LONG STREET, RIVERSIDE

Very Cool SPORTS

ARE YOU LOOKING FOR NEW SPORTS CLOTHES? ARE THE SPORTS STORES IN YOUR TOWN TOO EXPENSIVE?

We have thousands of

soccer shoes   sneakers   hoodies   swimsuits

shorts   T-shirts   gloves

for men, women, and children.

Visit our website!

RIVERSIDE MARKET

Shopping is fun at Riverside Market.

Saturdays and Sundays, 9:30–5:30

Clothes from around the world
Meat   Cheese   Games
Fruit   Toys   Books

18   B:29 **Listen. Where should they go?**

1 Amy _____   **2** Ben _____   **3** Fergus _____

19 **Write. Then ask and answer.**

1 Where can you buy toys?

_____

2 Where is Crazy Clothing?

_____

3 Where can you buy cheap sneakers?

_____

4 When can you buy food at Riverside Market?

_____

5 Can you shop online at Very Cool Sports?

_____

6 Can a man buy his clothes at Crazy Clothing?

_____

20 **What do you know?**

21 **Read. Then number.**

Choose the right shoes!

We all love wearing our favorite sneakers. But for some activities, sneakers aren't a good idea. Find out how to choose the right shoes.

1 In good weather, sneakers are great for walking in a city. But on a rainy day, your feet get wet. Sneakers are too soft for walking in the mountains. They can be dangerous. Always wear stiff walking shoes or boots.

3 For rock climbing, you want to feel the rock with your feet. Sneakers are too big for this. Climbing shoes are small and tight.

2 Dancers move and bend their feet a lot. The sneakers in this picture are good for dancers because the soles are soft in the middle. The soles of other sneakers are too stiff.

What shoes do you wear for your favorite sport?

22 **Read again and say** *walking, rock climbing,* **or** *dancing.*

1 You can't wear shoes with hard soles.
2 Your feet bend a lot.
3 The right shoes are very tight.
4 Soft shoes can be dangerous.

23 **Talk about the activities.**

A: I don't like rock climbing because it's too dangerous.
B: Really? I love rock climbing!

MINI PROJECT

24 **Design a pair of shoes.**

• **Think** about the shoes you have. What are they for? What activities do you like? What shoes do you need to do it?

• **Plan** a perfect pair of shoes for an activity. Think about the soles, laces, weight, and what they are made of.

• **Write** about the shoes' features and why you chose them. Design and create a poster.

• **Share** your poster with the class.

25 B:31 🎧 Listen and check (✓).

1 ⓐ ☐   ⓑ ☐   **2** ⓐ ☐   ⓑ ☐

3 ⓐ ☐   ⓑ ☐   **4** ⓐ $200 ☐   ⓑ $60 ☐

26 B:32 🎧 Listen and number the three things they buy.

ⓐ ☐   ⓑ ☐   ⓒ ☐   ⓓ ☐   ⓔ ☐   ⓕ ☐

27 Look at Activity 26. Use the key to ask and answer.

Key:
1 = $95.50
2 = $62.30
3 = $22.99

How much are the yellow sunglasses?

They're sixty-two dollars and thirty cents.

28 Write. Then role-play with a partner to check your answers.

Maddy: ¹_____ pens are these? And ²_____ hoodie is ³_____?

Robbie: They're not mine. Are ⁴_____ Emma's?

Maddy: No, they're not ⁵_____. Maybe they're Dan's? Hey, Dan. Are these ⁶_____ pens? And ⁷_____ this your ⁸_____?

Dan: Let's see... Oh, yes, the pens are ⁹_____, thanks. But the hoodie ¹⁰_____ mine.

Maddy: Well, ¹¹_____ hoodie is it? It's ¹²_____ big for a student.

Robbie: I don't know. Let's ask Mr. Smith. Maybe it's ¹³_____.

I CAN

I can ask and answer about how much things cost. ☐ ☐ ☐
I can ask and answer about who things belong to. ☐ ☐ ☐
I can write about a pair of shoes I have designed. ☐ ☐ ☐

Can assess what I have learned in Unit 5

29 Play the game.

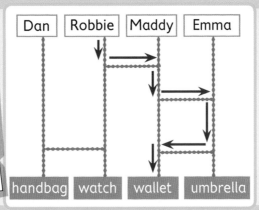

How to play

Start at the top and follow the lines until you get to the bottom. Change direction when you get to another line. You can only go down, right, or left, never up! Match the names at the top with the items at the bottom.

| Dan | Robbie | Maddy | Emma |

handbag · watch · wallet · umbrella

Whose handbag is it?
It's _____.
Whose watch is it?
It's _____.
Whose umbrella is it?
It's _____.
Whose wallet is it?
It's _____.

30 Play again and say. You can add extra lines to change the game. Add your own names for Number 4.

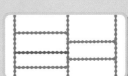

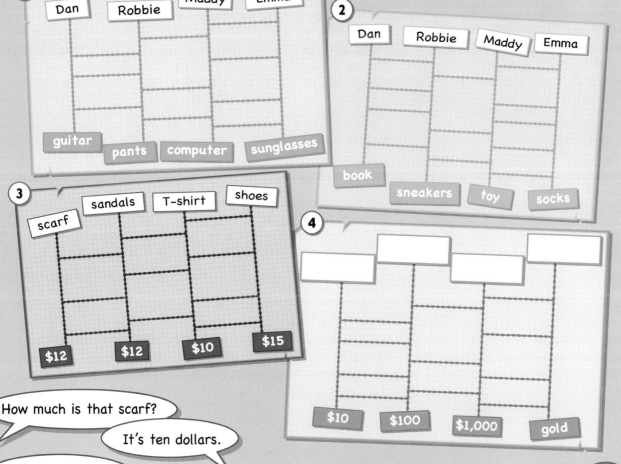

1 Dan · Robbie · Maddy · Emma

guitar · pants · computer · sunglasses

2 Dan · Robbie · Maddy · Emma

book · sneakers · toy · socks

3 scarf · sandals · T-shirt · shoes

$12 · $12 · $10 · $15

4

$10 · $100 · $1,000 · gold

How much is that scarf?

It's ten dollars.

Whose gold is it?

It's mine!

31 ⭐ I want to know more!

Now go to Poptropica English World

Lesson 10

Can use what I have learned in Unit 5

69

Wider World 3
Shopping for food

1 What do you know?

2 Listen and read. Then underline the foods.

1

Bao's blog

In Vietnam, we buy our food at the floating market. It opens at four o'clock in the morning. There are a lot of boats and you can climb from one boat to another to buy things. You can buy fish, rice, coconuts, bananas, … and snakes, too! Some of the snakes can dance. I love watching them. Some people buy snakes for dinner but I don't eat snakes – they're too expensive.

Bao, 12, Vietnam

2

Silvia's blog

In Buenos Aires, Argentina, there are some amazing bakeries. You can buy a lot of different pastries there. There's a lot of *dulce de leche* or milk caramel in the pastries. I often go to a bakery after school with my friends. Pastries are my favorite food.

Silvia, 11, Argentina

Can understand texts about shopping for food

Lily's blog

I live in the United Kingdom. My family doesn't buy fruit – we grow it in our yard. It's too cold for bananas, but we have a plum tree and two apple trees in our yard. In the spring and summer, we grow vegetables in the garden, too. There are some chickens in the yard and we eat their eggs. They love eating our vegetable seeds!

Lily, 12, United Kingdom

3 Circle. Check with a friend.

1 The floating market opens in the (morning / evening).
2 You can buy (snakes / cakes) at the floating market.
3 Silvia (always / often) goes to a bakery after school.
4 *Dulce de leche* means (milk caramel / sweet bakery).
5 Lily gets her fruit from the (yard / supermarket).
6 Chickens love eating (eggs / vegetable seeds).

4 Listen and check (✓). Who do you think said it?

	1	2	3	4	5	6
Bao						
Silvia						
Lily						

5 Ask and answer.

1 Where does your family buy food?
2 Are there any markets in your town? What do they sell?
3 Do you grow any food at home?

6 Write.

My favorite place to buy food is…

YOUR TURN!

- Plan the food for a party with a friend. Don't forget drinks and dessert.
- How many people are coming to the party? How much food will you need?
- Make a shopping list and note where you will buy or find each food.
    Cake (bakery)
    Apple juice (supermarket)
    Strawberries (garden)
- Tell the class.

6 Party time

 1 ⭐ **What do you know?**

 2 🎧 **B:35** **Listen and read. Why is there a cake?**

Yesterday, we had a big birthday party for Grandpa. My family came to our house and gave Grandpa a lot of presents.

1 My aunts brought some food and my mom made a big cake.

2 Please take the cake into the living room.

Sure, Mom.

3 I was taking the cake into the living room when I tripped and fell!

4 Argh!

We sang happy birthday, but we didn't eat cake!

 3 🎧 **B:36** **Listen and say.**

1  make/made

2  have/had

3 come/came

4 give/gave

5 get/got

6 sing/sang

7 bring/brought

8 meet/met

9 eat/ate

10 see/saw

 4 **Read and say. Use words from Activity 3.**

Maddy   Maddy's aunts   Mom   the family

The family gave Grandpa presents.

Can use irregular verbs to talk about the past

5   **Listen and write.**

LOOK!

I made a cake.

I didn't make a cake.

This is a picture of your Aunt Susan's birthday 40 years ago. She was 11 and we **¹**_____ a small party at home. Those are her friends, Robert and Tracey. They **²**_____ her a great present and we **³**_____ her a bicycle – she really **⁴**_____ a lot of presents! The girl with me is your mom. She was only five then. Those good-looking young people are your grandma and me. Yes, we were only 35! Your grandma **⁵**_____ a big chocolate cake. And that baby in her arms is your Uncle David. He **⁶**_____ a lot of cake that day. What a mess!

Grandparents (35)

Mom (5)

Uncle David (1)

Aunt Susan (11)

Robert and Tracey (10)

6 **Look at Activity 5 and say.**

1 Susan's family... (have)
2 Aunt Susan... (get)
3 Robert and Tracey... (bring)
4 Maddy's grandparents... (give)
5 Maddy's grandma... (make)
6 Uncle David... (eat)

Susan's family had a party.

7 **Look at Activity 5. Play True or False.**

a doll   Maddy's mom   pizza
strawberry cake   Susan
Susan's friends   the baby   the family

A: The baby didn't eat chocolate cake.
B: False! The baby ate chocolate cake.

Can talk about what did or didn't happen in the past

73

8 **B:39** Listen and say. Then write.

1st first **2**nd second **3**rd third **4**th fourth **5**th fifth ____th sixth **7**th seventh

8th eighth **9**th ninth **10**th tenth ____th eleventh **12**th twelfth **13**th thirteenth

14th fourteenth ____th fifteenth **16**th sixteenth **17**th seventeenth **18**th eighteenth ____th nineteenth

20th twentieth **30**th thirtieth

TIP!

twenty-first, twenty-second, twenty-third...
thirty-first, thirty-second, thirty-third...

  9 **B:40/ B:41** Listen to the song and write.

SONG

It was the ¹ _____ of December, snowy and white.

I ² _____ to a party that cold winter's night.

We danced, ³ _____, ⁴ _____, and had fun.

There were games. There were drinks for everyone.

Then... 10, 9, 8, 7, 6, 5, 4, 3, 2, 1...

It was 12 o'clock! Another new year!

We said ⁵ _____ to the old year.

We said ⁶ _____ to the new.

My friends, new and old, said,

"Happy New Year!"

"Happy New Year!" I said, too.

 10 **B:42** Listen, repeat, and say the next date.

1	February **22**nd	2	April **14**th
3	November **1**st	4	July **31**st
5	September **19**th	6	March **23**rd

 February twenty-second, February twenty-third

11 B:44 **Read. Then listen and write the dates.**

This diary belongs to: Jenny Amoako

 LOOK! B:43

Where did you go?	I went to Ghana.
When did you go to Ghana?	I went on August 1st.
What did you see?	I saw giant butterflies.
Who did you meet?	I met my relatives.

August

1st	I went to Ghana and met my relatives from Africa for the first time.
_____	I went to Kakum National Park and saw beautiful giant butterflies.
_____	I went to a soccer game in Accra. Ghanaians love soccer! I danced and sang soccer songs with my new friends.
10th	I went to the north of Ghana. I saw the giant baobab trees and ate some baobab fruit, but I didn't like it!
_____	I went to Lake Volta and sailed in a pirogue, a type of boat. It was cool!
_____	We had a party. My African friends gave me a lot of presents. "Come back soon!" they said. I cried at the airport.
_____	I came back home! I brought lots of presents for my mom, dad, and brother. It was a great experience!

12 **Look at Activity 11. Ask and answer.**

1 She... (meet)   **2** She... (see)
3 She... (dance)   **4** She... (sing)
5 She... (eat)   **6** She... (have)
7 She... (come)   **8** She... (bring)

When did she go to Ghana?

She went on August 1st.

15 **Read the story again. Then write correct sentences.**

1 Smith created a story about a lion and a tiger.

_____

2 The man pushed Polly into the snow.

_____

3 A polar bear tore Smith's pants.

_____

4 Hector Frost's pet wolf wears blue ribbons.

_____

5 The Police Chief's logo is on Smith's pants.

_____

6 The Police Chief wants Polly and Mike to go to the lake with her.

_____

16 **Role-play the story.**

17 **How good are you at solving problems? Talk about a solution for each problem.**

VALUES

Be a creative problem solver.

Problem 1
You don't know the meaning of a word.

Problem 2
You wore your friend's shirt and it got a mark which won't wash out.

Problem 3
You want to make friends at school, but you're shy.

HOME SCHOOL LINK

Tell a family member about a problem you solved at school.

I don't know the meaning of this word. What should I do?

You could look it up in a dictionary.

18 **Read. Was yesterday fun for Harry?**

Sally's Welcome Party

Who? Sally's friends, classmates, and teachers

Where? Hope School

When? Saturday, April 18th

What time? 6:30–9:00 p.m.

Harry's blog

Sunday, April 19th

Yesterday, we had a welcome party for Sally, a new student at school. Before the party, I went to my friend Mark's house for pizza. Then we went to school together in his dad's car. We saw all our friends there. Sally's parents were there, too. There was cool music but the room was too hot. We talked and played games. Then there was a dancing competition. A lot of the girls were good at dancing and Mark was good, too. He and Sally got a prize! We had a lot of fun!

19 **Circle.**

1   The party was at (school / Mark's house).
2   Harry met Mark (before / after) the party.
3   The party was on (Saturday / Sunday).
4   There was good (food / music) at the party but the room was too (hot / cold).
5   The children (talked / ate), played, and danced.
6   (Mark / Harry) and Sally got a prize.

20 **Listen and write.**

1   Who is talking?   _____
2   What did she eat before the party?   _____
3   Was she good at her favorite game?   _____
4   What did they do in the car on the way home?   _____

21 **Imagine you are Mark. Talk about the party.**

> Harry was at my house before the party.

22 **What do you know?**

23 **B:48** **Read. Then act out the mini-play in class.**

MINI-PLAY
The First Thanksgiving

In 1620, 102 settlers went from England to North America.

Look at our ship. It's called the Mayflower. It was our home for many weeks.

Now we have a new home. But we have no food! And it's the fall! There is no time to grow food before the winter!

The settlers' first winter in North America was very cold and snowy.

 I'm hungry.

 I'm scared!

In the spring, some Native Americans went to see the settlers.

You have no food. We are good at fishing and farming. We can help you.

Thank you!

Please teach us!

The Native Americans taught the settlers about growing food in their country.

It is the fall again. We have a lot of food now.

We must remember to give thanks. Let's celebrate Thanksgiving every year!

24 **Circle T = True or F = False. Then correct the false sentences.**

1   The Mayflower was a ship.   T / F
2   The settlers were from
    North America.   T / F
3   Their first months in North
    America were fun.   T / F
4   The Native Americans were
    good farmers.   T / F
5   The Native Americans taught
    the settlers to cook.   T / F
6   There was a lot of food at
    the first Thanksgiving.   T / F

MINI PROJECT

25 **Write a mini-play.**

• **Think** What special celebrations do you have in your country?

• **Plan** Work in a group and choose one. Think about how you celebrate it. Find out about the history of this celebration. When did it start? Why did it start?

• **Write** Write a mini-play about the history of this celebration.

• **Share** Act out your mini-play in class.

26 B:49 🎧 **Listen and number.**

a BASEBALL speed 10
Yes, Yes, Yes!
at bat

b

c

d

e

27 🗨 **Tell the story in Activity 26 to a friend.**

28 B:50 🎧 **Read and listen. Then write. Check your answers in pairs.**

I play basketball. My team is called Yellow Birds. On Saturday, it was the last game of the season. Before the game, my team had **94** points and were second in the league. Brown Bears were first. But because we won our last game, we went to first with **97** points. Brown Bears were second with **96** points. Blue Ducks were fourth before the last game on Saturday. They beat Red Cats so they went up to third with **80** points. Red Cats went down from fourth to fifth and ended with **78** points. Green Tigers were last in the league with only **70** points because they lost to Silver Snakes on Saturday. Silver Snakes went up to fourth with **79** points.

	TEAM NAME	POINTS	POSITION
1	Red Cats	78	
2	Green Tigers		
3	Brown Bears	96	2nd
4	Silver Snakes		
5	Yellow Birds		
6	Blue Ducks		

I CAN

I can use irregular verbs to talk about the past.
I can use ordinal numbers as dates.
I can write a mini-play.

29 **Can you read the messages? Write.**

CODE 1: DZ GXF X QAK MXLSC

1	2	3	4	5	6	7	8	9	10	11	12	13	14	15	16	17	18	19	20	21	22	23	24	25	26
A	B	C	D	E	F	G	H	I	J	K	L	M	N	O	P	Q	R	S	T	U	V	W	X	Y	Z
																					O				

Example: the twenty-second letter is really the fifteenth ➜ code letter V = O

The fourth letter is really the twenty-third.

The sixth letter is really the fourth.

The thirteenth letter is really the sixteenth.

The last letter is really the fifth.

The seventeenth letter is really the second.

The twelfth letter is really the eighteenth.

The seventh letter is really the eighth.

The first letter is really the ninth.

The nineteenth letter is really the twentieth.

The twenty-fourth letter is really the first.

The eleventh letter is really the seventh.

The third letter is really the twenty-fifth.

Message 1 =

CODE 2: XF BUF B MPU PG DBLF

1	2	3	4	5	6	7	8	9	10	11	12	13	14	15	16	17	18	19	20	21	22	23	24	25	26
A	B	C	D	E	F	G	H	I	J	K	L	M	N	O	P	Q	R	S	T	U	V	W	X	Y	Z

The second letter is the first.

The third letter is the second.

The fourth letter is the third, and so on.

Message 2 =

30 **Make your own code. Write a message to a friend.**

1	2	3	4	5	6	7	8	9	10	11	12	13	14	15	16	17	18	19	20	21	22	23	24	25	26
A	B	C	D	E	F	G	H	I	J	K	L	M	N	O	P	Q	R	S	T	U	V	W	X	Y	Z

Code

Message

31 **I want to know more!**

Now go to Poptropica
English World

Review Units 5 and 6

1 Choose a present. Write the letter. Then ask and answer.

Whose scarf is this? It's Uncle Andy's.

1 My grandparents often go to hot places.

2 My baby cousin, Ollie, likes animals.

3 Aunt Caroline loves baggy clothes.

4 My parents like sports and they love swimming.

5 Uncle Andy often goes to cold places. He likes skiing.

a $ ___.___

b $ ___.___

c $ ___.___

d $ ___.___

e $ ___.___

2 (B:51) Order the sentences in the dialog. Then listen and check.

a **Salesperson:** Yes, of course. Eighteen dollars and fifty cents, please.

b **Salesperson:** They're eighteen dollars and fifty cents.

c **Dan:** May I buy the pants, please?

d **Dan:** How much are those baggy pants?

3 Write prices for the items in Activity 1. Then role-play using the dialog in Activity 2.

Can talk about shopping and belongings

4 **Look and say.**

> Kathryn went to the United Kingdom on January tenth.

Kathryn Kelly

January	10th, the United Kingdom
February	
March	3rd, South Africa
April	
May	
June	22nd, Greenland
July	
August	31st, the United States
September	
October	5th, Italy
November	
December	19th, Australia

5 **Look and say.**

1 What did Kathryn do?
2 What was the problem?

> In the United Kingdom, she used many taxis. The problem was she wanted to walk but the evenings were too dark.

the United Kingdom / evenings / dark

the United States / horse / small

Australia / sun / hot

6 **Write.**

1 My sister _____ my lunch to me yesterday. (bring)
2 I _____ to the store and _____ a lot of clothes last week. (go / see)
3 I _____ my friends in the city last Saturday. (meet)
4 We _____ karaoke at school two days ago. (sing)

7 School

1 What do you know?

2 **B:52** Listen and read. Why are Emma and Robbie scared?

1. There was a story-writing competition at school today.

   Did you win?

   No, I didn't. My story wasn't very good. Writing a good story is difficult!

2. Dan was the winner. His story was about a green hand without a body.

   Was it scary?

   Of course it was scary! The green hand went to people's houses and...

3. Argh!

4. Ha, ha! Good joke, Dan!

   Dan! That wasn't funny!

3 **B:53** Listen and say.

1. interesting
2. boring
3. exciting
4. scary

5. funny
6. difficult
7. easy
8. romantic
9. relaxing

4 Talk about these things. Use words from Activity 3.

dark nights   math class   playing the piano
reading comic books   reading magazines   sci-fi movies
skateboarding   swimming   talking with friends   vacations

Talking with my friends is interesting.

Can use adjectives to describe experiences

B:54

Was it interesting?	Yes, it was. / No, it wasn't.
Was there an alien in it?	Yes, there was. / No, there wasn't.
Were there any exciting stories?	Yes, there were. / No, there weren't.

5 B:55 **Listen and ✓ or ✗.**

Story Competition Winners!

1 ISLAND ADVENTURE by James Duncan
2 MIKE GOES TO MARS by Isabella Brand
3 Nile Princess by Vinny da Souza

	1	2	3
exciting?	✓	✗	✓
scary?			
funny?	✗		✗
children?	✓	✓	
an alien?		✓	✗

6 **Look at Activity 5. Ask and answer.**

Was Mike Goes to Mars exciting?

7   **Look at Activity 5. Play the guessing game.**

No, it wasn't.

A: Was it exciting?
B: Yes, it was.
A: Were there any children in it?
B: Yes, there were.
A: It was *Island Adventure*!

8 **Listen and match. Then say.**

1. computer science
2. math
3. geography
4. science
5. history
6. art
7. music
8. P.E.

a b c d e f g h

9 B:57/ B:58 **Listen to the song and write.**

SONG

Chorus:
Math, ¹_____, history, ²_____, art, ³_____.
A lot of subjects every day. Is school boring? No way!
Last year, ⁴_____ wasn't easy. The lessons weren't always fun.
But now I can do all my homework. Math is for everyone!
(Chorus)
Last year, ⁵_____ was boring. P.E. lessons weren't my thing.
But now it's my favorite subject. I can play soccer and swim.
(Chorus)

10 **Look at Activity 9 and write. Then say and compare with a friend.**

Last year, math wasn't easy.

Jill

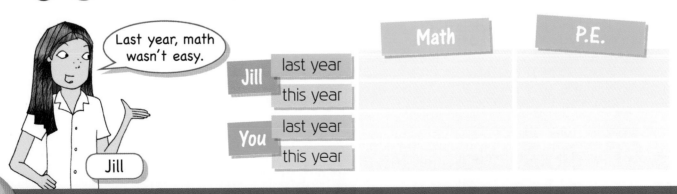

		Math	P.E.
Jill	last year		
	this year		
You	last year		
	this year		

B:59

Did you have computer science on Tuesday?	Yes, I did. / No, I didn't.
Was P.E. relaxing?	Yes, it was. / No, it wasn't. It was difficult.

11 **Listen and circle or write. Then ask and answer.**

B:60

	Monday	Tuesday	Wednesday	Thursday	Friday
Robbie	math	music	geography	English	history and art
	easy / difficult	easy / difficult	interesting / boring	easy / difficult	easy / difficult
Emma	_____	science	_____	computer science	_____
	difficult	_____	boring	interesting	_____

Did Robbie have music on Tuesday?

Was it easy?

Yes, he did.

No, it wasn't.

12 **Listen and write.**

B:61

1 Did Maddy have math homework on Monday?
Was it easy? _____
_____

2 Did she have art homework on Wednesday this week?
Was it boring? _____
_____

3 How about on Friday? What was her homework on Friday? _____
Was it difficult? _____

13 Talk about the pictures. Then listen and read.

14 Who dropped the piece of paper Polly picked up? Discuss your answers.

15 Read the story again. Then write.

1 Where does the tunnel go? _____
2 What does Polly find in the tunnel? _____
3 Which school subjects are part of the code? _____
4 When is science on the school schedule? _____
5 What is at 12:40 on the school schedule? _____
6 Why does Polly think there is a party at Bollington Hall? _____

16 Role-play the story.

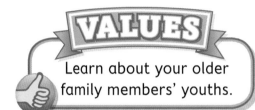

VALUES

Learn about your older family members' youths.

17 How much do you know about what your older family members were like when they were younger? Take the test. Then ask and answer.

Family member	I know! (score 2 points)	Score
1 For my _____,	school was (fun / boring).	
2 For my _____,	math (was / wasn't) easy.	
3 My _____	(was / wasn't) good at sports.	
4 My _____	(loved / hated) romantic movies.	
5 My _____	enjoyed (scary / funny) movies.	
6 For my _____,	_____ was relaxing.	
7 My _____'s	favorite food was _____.	
8 My _____'s	favorite movie star was _____.	
9 My _____'s	favorite singer/band was _____.	

My total score	/18

15–18 Very good! You know a lot.　　**10–14** Good! You know some things.
0–8 You should learn more. Find out when you get home today.

> For my mom, school was fun.

HOME SCHOOL LINK

Find out some other things about what your older family members were like when they were younger.

18 B:63 **Read. Then number.**

We love... SCHOOL TRIPS!

Where did you go on your last school trip?

a

b

c

1 Our science trip was exciting but scary, too. We went to a dark cave. There were lots of bats. They sleep inside the cave during the day and go out to eat at night.

Sam, 10, Seoul, Korea

2 Last fall, my class went on a history trip. We were looking at old buildings and learning about life 400 years ago. Our teacher said, "Take lots of pictures and write about the buildings." It was a fun day.

Luisa, 10, Lima, Peru

3 On Thursday, I went on a geography trip to a lake. The river in my city starts at this lake. We went to a waterfall, too. It wasn't very big but it was really beautiful. The water there is very clean.

Oliver, 11, Leeds, United Kingdom

  19 **Say True or False. Correct the false sentences.**

1 Sam's science trip was boring.
2 There weren't any animals in the cave.
3 Luisa went on a geography trip last fall.
4 Luisa learned about life 200 years ago.
5 Oliver and his class were in a city.
6 There was a beautiful waterfall near the lake.

> False. The science trip wasn't boring. It was exciting but scary.

   20 B:64 **Listen to the questions. Underline and number the answers in the blog.**

21 **Look at Activity 18. Talk about the trips.**

> Luisa's trip was interesting. I like old places.

22 **What do you know?**

23 **Read. Who were Tara's friends?**
B:65

Star Interview!

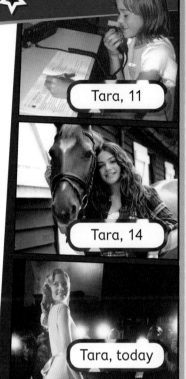

A lot of people know about your life as a movie star in Hollywood. But where was your home when you were a child?

In the middle of the desert in Australia. It was 200 kilometers from other children and 500 kilometers from a city!

Was it very boring?

No, it wasn't. It was interesting. There were horses on our farm and we also had a pet kangaroo. The animals were my friends. I still find riding horses relaxing today.

Where was your school?

I didn't have classes at school. My teacher was on a radio in the city and I was on a radio at home. There were other students on the radio, too, and every year there was a big party in the city. I was shy with the other children but it was always a very exciting day.

Tara, 11

Tara, 14

Tara, today

24 **Ask and answer.**

1   Was Tara's first home in Hollywood?
2   Were there any animals on her farm?
3   Were her classes in the city?
4   Was there a teacher?
5   Was there a party every month?
6   Were the parties exciting?

25 **Imagine you live in Tara's first home. Ask and answer.**

1   Is your life interesting?
2   Who are your friends?
3   What do you do every day?
4   Do you like your classes?
    Why? / Why not?

 MINI PROJECT

26 **Compare your school life with your grandparents'.**

• **Think** about your grandparents' school lives. How do you think they were different to yours?

• **Plan** by making a note of six questions to ask your grandpa or grandma. Think about school subjects, teachers, classrooms, and what students used (pens, books, computers).

• **Write** your questions and then interview your grandpa or grandma. Make a chart comparing your school life with his/hers.

• **Share** your chart with the class.

27 Listen and write. Check your answers in pairs.

	Monday	Tuesday	Wednesday	Thursday	Friday
1st class	[science]	ABC		ABC	
2nd class	English	[science]	1 + × % 2 − ÷ √	1 + × % 2 − ÷ √	
3rd class	1 + × % 2 − ÷ √	1 + × % 2 − ÷ √	[globe]		1 + × % 2 − ÷ √
	LUNCH				
4th class	[globe]		[art]	[music]	[art]
5th class	[history]			[sports]	

28 Listen. Then ask and answer.

> boring   funny   relaxing   romantic   scary
> Was it   Was there a   Were there any

Was it a funny story?

No, it wasn't.

29 Unscramble to make questions and match. Then ask and answer.

1 go / did / into / you / cave / the

_____

a Yes, there were. It was exciting!

2 bats / any / there / were

_____

b Yes, we did. It was dark and wet.

3 boat / was / a / there

_____

c Yes, we went to a lake near the cave.

4 go / any / did / places / you / other / to

_____

d No, there wasn't.

I CAN

I can use adjectives to describe experiences.
I can ask and answer using *Was it...* , *Was there...* , and *Were there...* ?
I can talk about my grandparents' school life.

30 Find and circle eight school subjects. The letters that are left tell you the answer!

G	E	O	G	R	A	P	H	Y
C	O	M	P	U	T	E	R	I
L	S	C	I	E	N	C	E	I
M	A	T	H	K	E	M	U	S
S	C	I	E	N	C	E	I	C
A	N	H	I	S	T	O	R	Y
A	R	T	D	M	U	S	I	C
S	C	I	P	E	E	N	C	E

What are your favorite school subjects?

_____
_____

31 Look at each picture and role-play a dialog. Take turns being Alison, Mark, Sue, Tim, Brett, and Julia.

Vacation Pictures!

1

Alison went on a rollercoaster.

A: Hi Alison. Where did you go?
B: I went to Brazil!
A: What did you do?
B: I went on a rollercoaster!
A: Was it exciting?
B: No! It was scary!

2

Mark climbed a wall.

3

Sue floated on a raft.

4

Tim saw a clown.

5

Brett played games.

6

Julia went to a museum.

32 I want to know more!

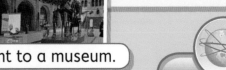

Now go to Poptropica English World

Wider World 4
Unusual schools

1 What do you know?

2 🎧 B:68 Listen and read. Then number the pictures.

a

b

c

1

Kai's blog

My new school in Tokyo is great. It's international so I have friends from 40 different countries! We learn a lot about other countries and cultures. It's so interesting. They always speak to me in English – their English is great. I'm learning Japanese. It was difficult at first but my friends were patient when I said the wrong words. Now it's easy.

Kai, 12, Japan

2

Abi's blog

I love my school! I go to a special school in the mountains. Students go there to study winter sports. Every day, after studying geography, math, and other subjects, we do sports for three hours. We go skiing and snowboarding. Some students from our school went to the Olympics. I want to be a famous skier, too.

Abi, 14, Canada

Can understand texts about unusual schools

 3 **Ask and answer.**

1 Who lives in a school?
2 Who is learning Japanese?
3 Who does sports for three hours a day?
4 Who has friends from 40 countries?

 4 **Ask and answer.**

1 Which school in Activity 2 do you want to go to? Why?
2 What do you like about your school?

 5 **What is important about school for you? Tell a friend.**

• good friends
• a swimming pool
• good teachers
• a lot of sports
• students from other countries

> A swimming pool is important for me because I like swimming.

Matu's blog

I live in my school because it's a boarding school. My friends and I all live in rooms next to the school. I love living with my friends because I never get lonely and we have lots of fun together. The teachers are all very nice and patient. In the evening, there are a lot of activities. We can watch movies, play tennis, or go swimming but usually we have homework.

Matu, 12, Kenya

YOUR TURN!

• Think about your ideal school. How is it different from your school now?
• Make notes on your ideal school's subjects, sports, teachers, and number of students.
• What else is special about your ideal school? *There is a rock climbing wall. / We watch a movie once a week.*
• Tell the class.

5 **Write.**

At my ideal school…

1 What do you know?

2 **C:02** Listen and read. Is Carlos playing?

1

Where's Carlos?

2

Who's Carlos? Where's he from?

He's a famous Spanish player. He was on an American team before and on an Italian team last year. Now he plays here, but he isn't in this game.

3

Maybe he was better before.

4

I am a good player. But look at my leg.

3 **C:03** Listen and say.

1 Chinese	**2** Korean	**3** Japanese	**4** Australian
5 American	**6** Mexican	**7** Colombian	**8** Brazilian
9 Argentinian	**10** British	**11** Spanish	**12** Italian
13 Egyptian	**14** Indian		

4 Talk about famous people from different countries.

Justin Timberlake is American.

Lionel Messi is Argentinian.

LOOK!

C:04

Is he/she from the United States?	Yes, he/she is.	No, he/she isn't.
Where's he/she from?	He's/She's from Argentina.	He's/She's Argentinian.
Where are they from?	They're from Australia.	They're Australian.

5 C:05 **Listen and match. Then ask and answer.**

International Singing Contest

a Colombia

b Spain

c the United States

d Mexico

e Japan

f Korea

Number 1. Where's he from?

He's from Spain. He's Spanish.

6 **Look at Activity 5 and play the game. True or False?**

A: Number 1. He's from Brazil.
B: False! He's from Spain. He's Spanish.
A: The Colombian flag is red, yellow, and green.
B: False! It's red, yellow, and blue.

7 **Listen and number. Then say.**

VOCABULARY

a  ☐
cowboy

b  ☐
king

c  ☐
queen

d  ☐
scientist

e  ☐
spy

f  ☐
soldier

g  ☐
sailor

h  ☐
waiter

i  ☐
actor

j  ☐
musician

TIP!

in	**in** the morning
	in May
	in the spring
	in 2015
on	**on** Thursday
	on January 16th
at	**at** five o'clock
	at night

8 **Listen to the song and write.**

SONG

¹_____ Friday, I was a cowboy.
²_____ Thursday, a Spanish king.
³_____ June, I was a waiter,
And a sailor ⁴_____ the spring.
Chorus:
I'm an ⁵_____, yes, an ⁶_____.
Acting's the life for me.
I'm an ⁷_____, yes, an ⁸_____.
Acting's the life for me.

⁹_____, I was a ¹⁰_____,
And a ¹¹_____. That was great!
I was a famous British ¹²_____,
In two thousand and eight.
(Chorus)
I get up at five ¹³_____ the morning.
My days are very long.
But a life in movies is exciting.
That's why I'm singing this song.
(Chorus)

9 **Look at Activity 8 and say. Use *in*, *on*, or *at*.**

1 waiter / June
2 sailor / the spring
3 famous spy / 2008
4 king / Thursday
5 gets up / five o'clock
6 cowboy / Friday

He was a waiter in June.

98 **Lesson 3** Can identify different occupations and use *in*, *on*, and *at* correctly

LOOK!

He's a cowboy.	He likes playing the guitar.	He's a cowboy **who** likes playing the guitar.
It's an American movie.	It's very famous.	It's an American movie **that**'s very famous.

10 Read and write.

1 This movie is about a Japanese scientist. She went to the moon. This movie is about a Japanese scientist _____ went to the moon.

She made a rocket. The rocket went to the moon.
She made a rocket _____ went to the moon.

2 This movie is about a French chef. He made cakes.
This movie is about a _____ who _____ .

He made a wedding cake. It was very big.
He made a _____ that _____ .

3 This movie is about an American waiter. He worked hard.
This movie is about _____ _____ .

He opened a restaurant. It was the best restaurant in New York.
He opened a _____ _____ in New York.

11 Listen and number. Then say.

C:10

He's the king who's eating.

12 Play the game. Think of a famous person and give hints to your partner.

14 Hector and Smith don't run away when they first see the police officers. Why not? Discuss your answers.

Can understand a simple story / Can discuss a story

15 **Read the story again and circle.**

1 The Queen is at Bollington Hall (to find her diamonds / for a costume party / to buy a costume).

2 "Amusing" means (scary / funny / relaxing).

3 The (knight / astronaut / explorer) is English.

4 (Mike / Polly / The Police Chief) sees the diamond necklace first.

5 The diamond necklace is (on Mars / around the dog's neck / inside the ice wall).

6 The Queen says that the Ice Detectives are (interesting and amusing / brave and smart / extraordinary).

16 **Role-play the story.**

17 **Circle and write for yourself. Then ask and answer.**

VALUES

Be a good role model for others.

A good role model is someone...	Do you? Yes/No/Sometimes	Does your friend? Yes/No/Sometimes
1 who arrives (late / on time)		
2 who (listens / talks) more		
3 who (shares / doesn't share)		
4 who (works / doesn't work) hard at school		
5 who plays (before / after) doing homework		
6 who (helps / doesn't help) at home		
7 who (says / doesn't say) "please" and "thank you"		
8 who (thinks before doing / does before thinking)		

Do you arrive on time?

Yes, I do.

Talk to your parents about how they are role models for you.

18
C:12

a

Big Kids

Channel 1 at 6:00 p.m. on Tuesday, June 28th

In this Australian show, children do their parents' jobs for a week and their parents go to school. This week, a boy is a waiter in an expensive restaurant and his dad has some problems with his math homework. Very funny!

b

The Finton Files

Channel 3 at 7:30 p.m. on Wednesday, June 29th

Here's an exciting spy story with interesting characters, and the actors are great! It's about Harry Finton who was an American spy in Italy 70 years ago.

c

Dr. Glock

Channel 5 at 10:00 a.m. on Thursday, June 30th

A scientist and his alien pet go to sea with some sailors. There are a lot of bad shows for children in the morning, but this one is fantastic!

d

The Big Game

Sports Channel 1 at 3:00 p.m. on Saturday, July 2nd

The Los Angeles Lakers play the Chicago Bulls in the last game of the basketball season.

19
C:13
Look at Activity 18. Then listen and number.

20 **Write.**

1   Dr. Glock is a scientist _____ has a pet _____.
2   _____ was an American _____ who lived
    in _____.
3   The dad who isn't good at _____ is normally a _____.
4   The _____ game of the _____ season is
    _____ July 2nd.

21 **Look at Activity 18 and choose. Tell a friend.**

> I want to watch *Dr. Glock*. It's exciting.

22 What do you know?

23 C:14 Read. Then number.

a

The history of video games

Every year, there are new video games. But let's look at some of the old ones...

1 The first video games were American. Pong was new in **1972** and it was too big and expensive for people's homes. Two small white rectangles went up and down and a small white square went left and right. What was the game? Computer table tennis!

b

2 The Game Boy was Japanese. It was first in the stores in **1989**. It was small and there were a lot of good games for it. The games were black and white. Games with the character Mario were very successful.

c

3 The Wii was new in **2004**. In a lot of Wii games, you play with all your body and not just your fingers. Some sports games are very good exercise!

24 Ask and answer.

1 Were the first video games Japanese?
2 Was Pong cheap?
3 Were the first Game Boy games in color?
4 Were the Mario games successful?
5 Was the Wii in stores five years ago?
6 Do you play some Wii games with your whole body?

25 Talk about the video games that you play.

boring   difficult   easy   exciting   interesting

Do you play Wii games?

No, I don't. I think they're boring.

MINI PROJECT

26 Write about a video game.

- **Think** about a video game that you like. When was it new? Where was it made?

- **Plan** by making notes about how you play the game. Are there any characters? Is there a story?

- **Write** four or five sentences about the video game.

- **Share** your paragraph with the class.

27 C:15 **Listen and number. Check in pairs.**

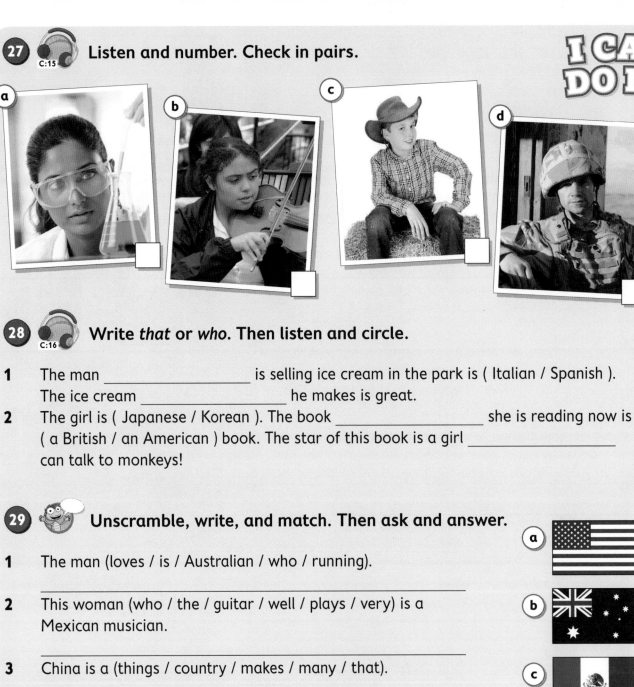

28 C:16 **Write *that* or *who*. Then listen and circle.**

1 The man _____ is selling ice cream in the park is (Italian / Spanish).
The ice cream _____ he makes is great.

2 The girl is (Japanese / Korean). The book _____ she is reading now is
(a British / an American) book. The star of this book is a girl _____
can talk to monkeys!

29 **Unscramble, write, and match. Then ask and answer.**

1 The man (loves / is / Australian / who / running).
_____

 a

2 This woman (who / the / guitar / well / plays / very) is a
Mexican musician.
_____

 b

3 China is a (things / country / makes / many / that).
_____

c

4 The United States is a (that / country / baseball / plays).
_____

 d

> What does the Australian man love?

> He loves running.

 **I CAN**

I can ask and answer about where someone is from.
I can talk about people and things using *who* and *that*.
I can write about a video game I like.

Can assess what I have learned in Unit 8

1 Your movie is...

exciting   funny   interesting   romantic   scary

2 Choose and describe three characters for your movie.

actor   cowboy   king   musician   queen
sailor   scientist   soldier   spy   waiter

1   Job: _____   Name: _____
2   Job: _____   Name: _____
3   Job: _____   Name: _____

Where are they from?
1 _____
2 _____
3 _____

What are they like?
1 _____
2 _____
3 _____

What do they look like?
1 _____
2 _____
3 _____

What are they good/bad at?
1 _____
2 _____
3 _____

3 What is your movie about? Tell the class.

_____
_____
_____
_____
_____
_____

My movie is very interesting. It is about a teacher who loves reading poetry. Her name is Rose and she is very beautiful. She has long, dark hair and green eyes. She is good at speaking other languages. She is Colombian but everyone thinks she's Italian. She helps an old explorer find treasure in a jungle!

31 I want to know more!

Now go to Poptropica English World

Review   Units 7 and 8

1 🎧 C:17 **Listen and match. Then ask and answer.**

School drama

1 Amy 2 Jill 3 Gemma 4 David 5 Fergus 6 Mike

king   queen   spy   scientist   sailor   soldier

2 **Write.**

When Amy's grandmother was young, school finished at age ¹_____. There ²_____ a long summer vacation and they went to school ³_____. There were some math, ⁴_____, geography, and history classes. P.E. was gym class but there ⁵_____ any English classes and of course, there weren't ⁶_____ computers in schools.

> Was there a queen in the drama?

> No, there wasn't.

> any   on Saturday   science
> wasn't   weren't   15

3 **Ask your parents about their schools. Write three questions.**

1 _____
2 _____
3 _____

Can talk about schools and school subjects

4 Write.

	Country	Nationality
1	He's from Argentina.	
2		She's Colombian.
3	They're from Italy.	
4		He's Egyptian.
5	They're from Brazil.	
6		She's Korean.
7	They're from Japan.	

5 C:18 Listen and write. Then say.

1 He's _an American soldier who wears a uniform_.
2 She's _____.
3 They were _____.
4 He's _____.
5 It's _____.
6 They're _____.

This is a soldier who is from the United States. He wears a uniform.

He's an American soldier who wears a uniform.

6 Think of animals or famous people. Write a quiz. Then ask a friend.

1 Is Jennifer Lawrence American? _____
2 Where are kangaroos from? _____
3 _____
4 _____
5 _____
6 _____
7 _____

Goodbye

1 🎧 C:19 **Listen and number.**

2 💬 **Ask and answer.**

1 What was your favorite scene in the story? Why?
2 Who was your favorite character in the story? Why?
3 What was your favorite song in this book? Can you sing it?
4 Which "*Have Fun*" page was the best in this book?

Can ask and answer about the story

3 Look and write. What unit are these pictures from?

Unit _____

Unit _____

Unit _____

Unit _____

Unit _____

4 Write. Who said it?

1 "Ah, those beautiful diamonds!"   _____

2 "Eat your breakfast, guys."   _____

3 "This is a job for the Ice Detectives."   _____

4 "The bear almost ate me."   _____

5 "A dog costume – how interesting!"   _____

5 Write the answers.

1 What's the name of the big house in the story?   _____

2 What's the name of the bald thief?   _____

3 What's the name of the thief who loves diamonds?   _____

4 What falls off a dog many times in the story?   _____

5 Who wants to go to the lake?   _____

6 Can Mike play soccer?   _____

7 What is Gizmo like?   _____

8 Is Smith good at working out?   _____

9 What does Polly hear at 2:00 a.m.?   _____

10 What is the code in the tunnel?   _____

6 Write. Ask a friend to read and comment.

_____ years ago I went to
_____
_____
_____

"I read this." Friend signs here:
_____
Friend's comment:
_____
_____
_____

7 Draw and write about your family, friends, and country. Then say.

My family

This is my _____
who is _____.
_____ can _____,
but can't _____.
_____ likes _____.

My friends

What are they good at?
_____
What are they like?
_____
What do they look like?
_____

My country

This is _____.
I'm _____.
It's a country that is famous for _____
_____.

8 Write a sentence from each unit to remind you of the language you learned in it.

Welcome Unit _____

Unit 1 _____

Unit 2 _____

Unit 3 _____

Unit 4 _____

Unit 5 _____

Unit 6 _____

Unit 7 _____

Unit 8 _____

Can use what I have learned

9 Write a country quiz. Then draw and color the flag.

1 This is a country that _____.

2 This is a country that _____.

3 This is a country that _____.

4 This is a country that _____.

5 This is a country that _____.

10 Write three rules for home and three rules for school. Use *must* and *should.*

My rules

At home

1 _____
_____
2 _____
_____
3 _____
_____

At school

1 _____
_____
2 _____
_____
3 _____
_____

11 Make a snowflake farewell card for your friends to sign.

First, get some paper and cut out a square.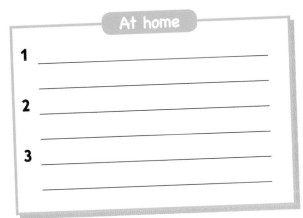

Second, fold it in half from corner A to corner C.

Third, fold it in half again from corner B to corner D.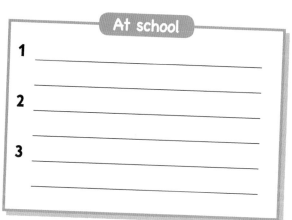

Fourth, fold corner A/C one third in.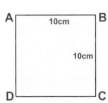

Fifth, do the same for corner B/D. It will go over the first fold.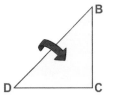

Sixth, cut off the top points at an angle.

Seventh, cut shapes into the sides of the triangle. Be creative!

It's a snowflake! Stick it onto a different color piece of paper.

Wordlist

Verb list

Present	Past	Past participle
act	acted	acted
agree	agreed	agreed
be: am/is/are	was/were	been
believe	believed	believed
beat	beat	beaten
blush	blushed	blushed
borrow	borrowed	borrowed
break	broke	broken
bring	brought	brought
brush	brushed	brushed
build	built	built
burn	burned	burned
buy	bought	bought
call	called	called
catch	caught	caught
chat	chatted	chatted
check	checked	checked
choose	chose	chosen

Present	Past	Past participle
clean	cleaned	cleaned
climb	climbed	climbed
clip	clipped	clipped
close	closed	closed
collect	collected	collected
comb	combed	combed
come	came	come
complain	complained	complained
complete	completed	completed
cost	cost	cost
count	counted	counted
cry	cried	cried
cut	cut	cut
dance	danced	danced
design	designed	designed
dig	dug	dug
do	did	done
download	downloaded	downloaded

Present	Past	Past participle
draw	drew	drawn
dress	dressed	dressed
drink	drank	drunk
dry	dried	dried
dust	dusted	dusted
eat	ate	eaten
empty	emptied	emptied
explain	explained	explained
fail	failed	failed
fall	fell	fallen
feed	fed	fed
feel	felt	felt
find	found	found
finish	finished	finished
fix	fixed	fixed
floss	flossed	flossed
fly	flew	flown
follow	followed	followed
forget	forgot	forgotten
frown	frowned	frowned

Present	Past	Past participle
get	got	gotten
give	gave	given
go	went	gone
hang	hung	hung
has/have	had	had
hear	heard	heard
help	helped	helped
hide	hid	hid
hit	hit	hit
install	installed	installed
join	joined	joined
jump	jumped	jumped
know	knew	known
laugh	laughed	laughed
lean	leaned	leaned
learn	learned	learned
leave	left	left
listen	listened	listened
live	lived	lived
look	looked	looked

Present	Past	Past participle	Present	Past	Past participle
lose	lost	lost	push	pushed	pushed
mail	mailed	mailed	put	put	put
make	made	made	rake	raked	raked
meet	met	met	read	read	read
memorize	memorized	memorized	rent	rented	rented
miss	missed	missed	rescue	rescued	rescued
mop	mopped	mopped	rest	rested	rested
move	moved	moved	return	returned	returned
open	opened	opened	ride	rode	ridden
pack	packed	packed	ring	rang	rung
paint	painted	painted	roast	roasted	roasted
pass	passed	passed	run	ran	run
pay	paid	paid	say	said	said
photograph	photographed	photographed	search	searched	searched
play	played	played	see	saw	seen
practice	practiced	practiced	sell	sold	sold
prepare	prepared	prepared	send	sent	sent
print	printed	printed	set	set	set
pull	pulled	pulled	shake	shook	shaken
pump	pumped	pumped	shoot	shot	shot

Present	Past	Past participle	Present	Past	Past participle
show	showed	shown	touch	touched	touched
sign	signed	signed	trade	traded	traded
sing	sang	sung	turn	turned	turned
sit	sit	sit	use	used	used
skate	skated	skated	visit	visited	visited
sleep	slept	slept	wait	waited	waited
solve	solved	solved	walk	walked	walked
stay	stayed	stayed	warm	warmed	warmed
study	studied	studied	wash	washed	washed
surf	surfed	surfed	watch	watched	watched
sweat	sweated	sweated	water	watered	watered
sweep	swept	swept	wear	wore	worn
swim	swam	swum	weed	weeded	weeded
take	took	taken	whistle	whistled	whistled
talk	talked	talked	win	won	won
tell	told	told	worry	worried	worried
text	texted	texted	wrap	wrapped	wrapped
think	thought	thought	write	wrote	written
throw	threw	thrown	yawn	yawned	yawned
tie	tied	tied	yell	yelled	yelled

Acknowledgments

The Publishers would like to thank the following teachers for their suggestions and comments on this course:

Nurhan Deniz, Alejandra Juarez, Lara Ozer, Cynthia Xu, Basia Zarzycka, Jamie Zhang

Jennifer Dobson, Anabel Higuera Gonzalez, Honorata Klosak, Dr Marianne Nikolov, Regina Ramalho

Hilda Martinez, Xochitl Arvizu, Tim Budden , Tina Chen, Betty Deng, Aaron Jolly, Dr. Nam-Joon Kang, Dr. Wonkey Lee, Wenxin Liang, Ann Mayeda, Wade O. Nichols

Asako Abe, JiEun Ahn, Nubia Isabel Albarracín, José Antonio Aranda Fuentes, Juritza Ardila, María del Carmen Ávila Tapia, Ernestina Baena, Marisela Bautista, Carmen Bautista, Norma Verónica Blanco, Suzette Bradford, Rose Brisbane, María Ernestina Bueno Rodríguez, María del Rosario Camargo Gómez, Maira Cantillo, Betsabé Cárdenas, María Cristina Castañeda, Carol Chen, Carrie Chen, Alice Chio, Tina Cho, Vicky Chung, Marcela Correa, Rosalinda Ponce de Leon, Betty Deng, Rhiannon Doherty, Esther Domínguez, Elizabeth Domínguez, Ren Dongmei, Gerardo Fernández, Catherine Gillis, Lois Gu, SoRa Han, Michelle He, María del Carmen Hernández, Suh Heui, Ryan Hillstead, JoJo Hong, Cindy Huang, Mie Inoue, Chiami Inoue, SoYun Jeong, Verónica Jiménez, Qi Jing, Sunshui Jing, Maiko Kainuma, YoungJin Kang, Chisato Kariya, Yoko Kato, Eriko Kawada, Sanae Kawamoto, Sarah Ker, Sheely Ker, Hyomin Kim, Lee Knight, Akiyo Kumazawa, JinJu Lee, Eunchae Lee, Jin-Yi Lee, Sharlene Liao, Yu Ya Link, Marcela Marluchi, Hilda Martínez Rosal, Alejandro Mateos Chávez, Cristina Medina Gómez, Bertha Elsi Méndez, Luz del Carmen Mercado, Ana Morales, Ana Estela Morales, Zita Morales Cruz, Shinano Murata, Junko Nishikawa, Sawako Ogawa, Ikuko Okada, Hiroko Okuno, Tomomi Owaki, Sayil Palacio Trejo, Rosa Lilia Paniagua, MiSook Park, SeonJeong Park, JoonYong Park, María Eugenia Pastrana, Silvia Santana Paulino, Dulce María Pineda, Rosalinda Ponce de León, Liliana Porras, María Elena Portugal, Yazmín Reyes, Diana Rivas Aguilar, Rosa Rivera Espinoza, Nayelli Guadalupe Rivera Martínez, Araceli Rivero Martínez, David Robin, Angélica Rodríguez, Leticia Santacruz Rodríguez, Silvia Santana Paulino, Kate Sato, Cassie Savoie, Mark Savoie, Yuki Scott, Yoshiko Shimoto, Jeehye Shin, MiYoung Song, Lisa Styles, Laura Sutton, Mayumi Tabuchi, Takako Takagi, Miriam Talonia, Yoshiko Tanaka, María Isabel Tenorio, Chioko Terui, José Francisco Trenado, Yasuko Tsujimoto, Elmer Usaguen, Hiroko Usami, Michael Valentine, José Javier Vargas, Nubia Margot Vargas, Guadalupe Vázquez, Norma Velázquez Gutiérrez, Ruth Marina Venegas, María Martha Villegas Rodríguez, Heidi Wang, Tomiko Watanabe, Jamie Wells, Susan Wu, Junko Yamaguchi, Dai Yang, Judy Yao, Yo Yo, Sally Yu, Mary Zhou, Rose Zhuang

Printed in Great Britain
by Amazon